Crisis

of

Skills

D0994966

Caring in Crisis

A Handbook of Intervention Skills for Nurses

Bob Wright SRN RMN
Senior Charge Nurse, Accident and Emergency Department,
Leeds General Infirmary, Leeds

Foreword by

Annie T. Altschul CBE
BA BSc RGN RMN RNT FRCN
Emeritus Professor of Nursing, University of Edinburgh;
Mental Health Adviser, World Health Organization

Churchill Livingstone 🏛

EDINBURGH LONDON MELBOURNE AND NEW YORK 1986

CHURCHILL LIVINGSTONE
Medical Division of Longman Group Limited

Distributed in the United States of America by Churchill Livingstone Inc.,
1560 Broadway, New York, N.Y. 10036, and by associated companies, branches and
representatives throughout the world.

First published 1986

ISBN 0 443 03354 4

British Library Cataloguing in Publication Data
Wright, Bob
  Caring in Crisis: a handbook for nurses.
  1. Diseases 2. Nursing
  I. Title
  616'.0024613 RT65

Library of Congress Cataloging in Publication Data
Wright, Bob, SRN, RMN.
  Caring in Crisis.
  Includes index.
  1. Intensive care nursing—Psychological aspects. 2. Critically ill—Psychology.
  3. Nurse and patient. 4. Nurses—Job stress.
  I. Title. (DNLM: 1. Crisis Intervention—nurses' instruction.
  2. Emergencies—nursing. WY 154 W947c)
  RT120.I5W75 1986 610.73'61 85-19552

Produced by Longman Singapore Publishers Pte Ltd.
Printed in Singapore

Foreword

Caring in Crisis is a book for nurses who work with the acutely ill and injured.

The author's long experience in such work tells him that many nurses at present are ill-equipped to deal with the emotional aspects of crisis which overwhelm victims, their nearest and dearest, and the nursing staff whose daily intense involvement in stressful situations can leave them drained or, in modern terminology, 'burnt-out'.

All nurses who work in hospitals for the critically and acutely ill will recognise the situations Bob Wright describes. They will readily identify with the people about whom he writes in his short, vivid, illustrative examples. They will experience a great sense of relief to realise that problems they had thought unique to themselves are shared by others, and to find that the validity of these problems is acknowledged.

I feel certain that the process of re-evaluation, advised by the author, will accompany the reading of this book, and that the new insight gained will result in a refreshed outlook on life and an enhanced capacity for caring.

In the future, one hopes, nurses will not be ill-equipped for the demanding work in acute and critical care areas. Their training will have prepared them to care for the whole patient, to cope with psychological problems, to evaluate themselves and to assist each other. This is the aim of all nursing education today, but in reality we

vi / Foreword

often only pay lip service to this. Textbooks and classroom teaching still deal in detail with physical care and offer little advice on the details of emotional and social aspects of caring.

This book could help all nurses, not only those whose immediate concern is with crisis care, to gain proper understanding of emotional problems. Every chapter deals with problems nurses meet in their own lives and with crises and disasters in the lives of their patients. Every chapter gives a detailed account of what these experiences mean to the sufferer and of the way some nurses have managed successfully to offer help.

What is so attractive about this book is that it does not exhort nurses to do this or that. It starts from the perspective of the sufferer, be this a patient, a relative or a nurse. When the reader has thought deeply about the way crisis has affected the situation, methods of intervention come to mind, helped in this book by sensitive suggestions and by the pervasiveness of the author's own humanity.

There are topics for further contemplation and discussion at the end of each chapter, but there are no easy solutions. Reading the book makes one feel good, even if in any particular situation, one may not have succeeded.

This book represents, in my opinion, a landmark in nursing literature. Bob Wright will earn the gratitude of the nursing profession for having helped to prevent burn-out instead of just describing and deploring it, and for making emotional crisis understandable and mangeable.

Edinburgh 1986   A.T.A.

Preface

I have been trying to sort out in my own mind why I have a particular interest in crisis care. My nursing career spans 20 years, and it was after about 16 years in nursing that I decided to study the problem more deeply. I believe the time was significant; having spent 8 years in acute care in psychiatric nursing and 8 years in general nursing where my experience was mostly in accident and emergency, I had gained an awareness and knowledge that frequently makes the picture complete for me, in my evaluation of a patient.

Separating the psyche from the soma makes me very uncomfortable as is the case for most nurses, but it is only in recent years that we have been actively encouraged to care for the whole patient. We may agree that this is the only approach but it is one fraught with difficulties. Because of old ideas and teaching practice, we may have concentrated too much on the organic problems of our patients, and may have difficulty in marrying their phsyical and emotional needs. Our encounter with areas of emotional need may open a floodgate of problems that overwhelm us. We may feel ill-prepared for the response we are faced with.

The people in the front line of health care are often ill-equipped to deal with crisis or psychiatric emergency. It seems incredible that we are equipped for the most serious medical emergency but not for the crisis that may accompany it. When this crisis occurs there is no way we can separate it from the emergency itself. All aspects of his response to the emergency or illness are an integral part of each patient.

In each chapter I have attempted to integrate the emotional crisis with the patient's physical condition. These chapters are by no means a comprehensive list of conditions having the potential to produce crisis, because this potential exists in all illness, accidents and conditions. The chapters deal with conditions which are more commonly seen.

The crises experienced by our patients are not limited to them. The crises become a part of our work, and, for a time, a part of us. It is hoped that we will emerge from these experiences as agents of care who are able to facilitate change and direction in crisis. Our increased effectiveness in these situations will mean we are more likely to emerge unscathed but with increased skills.

Our involvement in these areas of nursing, however, will also confront us with our own emotional needs. These experiences should, ideally, increase our insight into ourselves and into our strengths and weaknesses, but they can also create crisis. In the chapter on staff stress, I examine the way we nurses need to deal with our own crises, and become aware of the problem of 'burn-out'.

This book is based upon my experience in a district general hospital Accident and Emergency Unit, a travelling scholarship to the United States of America to study psychiatric nurse clinicians in emergency areas, and my psychiatric nursing experience. Some of the crisis experience was gained through extra counselling training in marital therapy, group work with adolescents, and clients with relationship difficulties.

It is important to me that my colleagues and management have given me the freedom to further my particular interest and that they continue to do so. The way that my individuality is recognised helps me to deal with the individuality of the patients I encounter.

The way in which I have been enabled to study this area of nursing care has given me an opportunity to look at other people's research, other nurses' ways of working, and ways to improve care in a crisis. I do not offer a blueprint that will be effective in every situation. I emphasise throughout the book that we are dealing with individuals who have unique experiences past and present.

The purpose of the book is to describe a theory about crisis and its process for nurses, and to focus on what happens to normal people, who ill or injured, develop a crisis or who, because they are in crisis, become ill or suffer injury. I have attempted to present the way I, as a nurse with long experience in acute care, see ways of intervening in the light of research by others. This may seem controversial and complex at times, but there are no neat, clear-cut directions for dealing with what we will encounter.

I hope you will be encouraged to help your patients/clients to find answers. In your attempt to do this, I know you will be surprised, hurt, enlightened and moved. I am constantly amazed, when patients and their families are faced with the most overwhelming diasters in their lives, at their strength and ability to move forward. They have much to teach us, both in our work and personal lives.

I would like to use this introduction to thank the many patients, staff members and colleagues in Britain and the USA who have taught and supported me, to thank Anne for typing and appraising my work, and, last but not least, to thank my wife and kids for their encouragement, support and keeping quiet when I needed them to.

Leeds 1986   B.W.

Contents

Contents

1

Crisis counselling and intervention

THE NATURE OF CRISIS

Before we look specifically at counselling and intervention we
should consider what a crisis is. The word itself conjures up
thoughts of major disaster such as a flood, famine or earthquake. It is commonly heard with reference to economic
situations and political problems, and in this sense the word
crisis has enormous organisational implications and suggests
that certain individuals or groups of people will have extreme
demands made upon them. What we do know is that a crisis
is a serious event which can have devastating implications.

For us, in the front line of illness, accidents and
emergencies, crisis assumes a much more personal meaning.
We may be faced with the patient, his family and friends
feeling totally overwhelmed and impotent, and being
disturbed by some very powerful feelings. This more individual application of the word brings it closer to our own
experience and makes 'crisis' more disturbing.

While stress may lead to a crisis, we must differentiate
between the two. Stress invokes tension and anxiety whereas
crisis is something which disturbs old habits and evokes the
potential for new responses. It it seen as bringing out the
potential for new responses. It is seen as bringing out the

mechanisms for coping. You will see that crisis is not necessarily a disastrous event. It can provide the opportunity for personal growth and development, and may lead to our having more effective coping mechanisms and thus increase our sense of well-being.

We cannot describe certain events and predict that they will lead to a crisis; often the response depends on how certain events are perceived. How we experience these events, understand them and cope with the feelings associated with them will determine whether a crisis will result. For some, e.g. a professional pianist, a laceration to the hand has overwhelming, all-embracing implications. For others, the death of a loved one can be painful and distressing but can also result in the gaining of personal strength and stature. We must avoid equating crisis with a catalogue of terrible events and must look beyond the events to the response.

Erikson (1950) describes life in adolescence as an unfolding sequence of crises which offers an opportunity for heightening potential. At this stage of increased vulnerability he describes the various periods as being critical. They are perceived as being moments between regression and progress. I believe it is important that we see any critical period, which occurs at any time of life, as having great potential for growth and forward movement. This applies not only to our clients but to ourselves.

Being aware that a stressful event may lead to a crisis, we must increase our own awareness of how it is perceived. Caplan (1964) defines a crisis as a threat, a call to new action, and a disturbance of habit. He then goes on to describe a process which gives us more indications as to the nature of the crisis, a process involving the life event, the individual's perception of the event and his ability to cope with it.

This process can therefore be a growth process or a destructive process which attacks self-esteem and ability to cope and leaves someone feeling damaged.

TYPES OF CRISIS

Crises are usually divided into two types: the coincidental and the developmental. Some life crises, however, such as sudden

Table 1.1

Coincidental (Accidental)	Developmental
Sudden illness	Birth
Accident	Puberty/adolescence
Redundancy	Courtship
Loss of income	Marriage
Loss of status	Pregnancy
Loss of security	Menopause
Divorce/separation	Death
	Sudden death

death, appear to fit into both categories. Table 1.1 shows how some of these life events fit into the two types of crisis.

These crises are all associated with a drastic change in social role. While many of the crises we are faced with are coincidental, they may also be associated with developmental crisis. An illness (coincidental) may exacerbate a developmental crisis. For example, an adolescent boy may have difficulty coping with changes in his body; his admission for an appendicectomy and the ensuing contact with young nurses may influence his thoughts and feelings about his image and his masculinity. The event — the appendicitis — which precipitated the feelings pales into insignificance when he becomes vulnerable because of his adolescent identity problems. It is therefore worth thinking about the stage someone has reached in his developmental life when he is having to face some illness or accident. If he is at a vulnerable stage, the 'stressor' (illness or accident) may lead to a crisis. The event in itself may be so overwhelming that it produces a coincidental crisis irrespective of the subject's developmental phase.

THE PHASES OF CRISIS

Caplan (1964) describes the four phases of crisis in which there can be resolution.

Phase One

A threatening situation occurs which disturbs the equilibrium. Past experiences are utilized but there is little or no experience of the event. The hazard is seen as a threat to the individual's basic needs. These may be love or ties of affection, or something else, the lack of which may threaten his very existence. In this impact phase there may be numbness and/or an inability to believe what is happening. Pain and anguish may then be experienced. These feelings may be internalised or may be discharged verbally or with tears and expressions of sorrow. He will try to think of ways of reducing the threat that he is experiencing.

Time becomes an important factor.

Phase Two

There is a strong desire or need to 'do something' about the situation. You will often hear the question 'What do you want me to do?' It is at this stage you begin to see some activity. Fear may be expressed or felt, along with feelings of helplessness and guilt. The feelings of ineffectiveness and lack of direction to move in are powerful and very distressing, and can produce agitation and restlessness. The increased activity may be a way of discharging anxiety. Quick solutions may be sought and it may be obvious to you that these have been chosen with little thought as to their effectiveness. They may not even be directed at helping the situation but may produce frantic disorganised activity. Successive 'trial and error' attempts, both in active and verbalised solutions, increase the sense of hopelessness and inadequacy. It is both demoralising and defeating to have little or no control over what is important to you.

Remember that time remains an important factor.

Phase Three

As the individual moves into this phase, you will see a continued rise in tension. There will be periods of intense activity to try to resolve the situation. Old resources are recalled in an attempt to find a solution and this causes an additional problem at this stage. The resurrection of old resources highlights old anxieties.

You will become aware of a shift of focus to previous painful and difficult situations. This shift of focus may offer a refuge away from the painful reality of the immediate problem. The strength of feelings aroused by the old anxiety interferes and distorts the present crisis. As well as this shift from the main problem to previous anxieties you may begin to see a shift to some trivial aspect of the present situation.

Panic and bewilderment are brought about by the absence of solution and resolution. This may result in noisy and erratic outbursts of behaviour.

Remember the time factor. How can anyone cope with this intensity of feeling for much longer?

Phase Four

In this phase the patient or client can no longer endure the distress. Denial and/or withdrawal may occur and you may have difficulty making contact or gaining access. This withdrawal or denial is particularly disturbing to the family as well as to the nurse. It is often perceived that the individual has 'gone mad' or will be permanently damaged. A compounding factor may be that this person is perceived as a 'key person' by the rest of the family. Traditionally or characteristically it is this person who has usually assumed leadership or sorted out family problems.

The family or individual is said to be more susceptible to intervention in Phase Two.

To summarise so far

A crisis occurs when an individual is faced with an insurmountable obstacle which is important to his life's aims and which threatens his very existence. The usual methods of problem solving are ineffective and the person becomes disorganised. Intense efforts are made to solve the problem and past anxieties interfere with the individual's ability to organise himself. Intervention should deal with the immediate crisis and he will need your help to do this. Before dealing with the crisis it will be ascertained that the individual concerned has no known classification of mental illness.

Each phase describes a level of the crisis. The four phases of crisis are summarised in Figure 1.1. The times on the clock are not significant in themselves but serve as a reminder that

Phase One
A threatening situation occurs
A threat to individual's needs
Produces tension, discomfort, strain, stress
Past experiences utilised to produce resolution

Phase Two
Past experiences fail to resolve crisis
Tension not only persists but increases
This generates feelings of helplessness
This encourages trial and error attempts to resolve problem

Phase Three
Trial and error attempts fail
Rising tension and disorganisation
Intensive periods of activity
Old anxieties recur
Trivial aspects may be dwelt upon
The 'make or break' phase

Phase Four
All attempts have failed
Feels helpless and hopeless
Tensions above coping threshold
May cause major breakdown such as depression

Fig. 1.1 The crisis process

time is an important factor and becomes more disruptive during the later phases of the crisis.

A summary of the phases illustrating the level of crisis is shown in Table 1.2. This also helps to define the focus in each phase. Each phase, therefore, describes a level of crisis.

Table 1.2

Phase	Intervention
Phase One	May be resolved by routine coping mechanisms
Phase Two	May be resolved by trying on a trial and error basis
Phase Three	May be resolved by redefining the situation or the motives of the individual, or both
Phase Four	Is a description of a severe state of crisis where an individual has insufficient resources to cope

CRISIS COUNSELLING

Before I begin to discuss how we deal with the crisis I would like to consider the word 'counselling'. The major problem about this word is that it is often used inappropriately. You will sometimes hear about a nurse being counselled when disciplinary measures are being taken. Although we are unable to examine the nature of counselling in any depth, we must stress that it is totally removed from anything of a punitive nature.

As far as the nurse is concerned, the task of counselling involves exploring and examining the present situation with the patient and/or his family. This is not an intellectual exercise but must involve the feelings of the patient/client and this is undertaken by helping him to feel safe with you. The hospital, and you as its representative, may be perceived as a threat for many reasons. Being in uniform, for example, may cause some difficulty about your being recognised as an individual. You may be seen as someone who will defend and promote the institution (hospital) above all else. It is hoped that your empathy and individuality will help you to understand the patient's difficulties and feelings.

Firstly, you have on offer your own humanity. In my view this comes before your role as nurse. Your being a nurse may interfere with the transaction, and your concern for the pain, distress and difficulty needs to be communicated both verbally and physically. Many nurses deny or are diffident about the skills they have to offer. To deny any ability or skill is as unrealistic as feeling able to sort out any problem.

A desire to see a solution quickly will cause you problems. In a busy ward or department, time can become an all-important factor. When you believe in the real value of the intervention you will feel less threatened by the time factor.

Giving advice which the individual is unable to carry out is to be avoided. It will increase your sense of inadequacy and is not useful. Your acceptance of the individual and what he or the family brings is of immense value. You do not have to agree with the lifestyle or morals or behaviour of the patient or his family. You are responding to emotional anguish, pain and distress. Because of strong personal feelings there may be occasions when someone else should be involved. This may occur if you have strong religious or ethical values which may be compromised. If you are unable to opt out of the situation, you will need to be aware of the possibility of these values interfering inappropriately with the transaction. This can be very difficult. Imagine having to treat the self-poisoned child rapist or murderer. The feelings produced can be so powerful as to be overwhelming. It is in this situation you become most aware of the value of space ('time out') to discharge feelings and air views after the event.

Never underrate the value of being a good listener. Stay with the patient and/or his family, and their feelings. Can you remember being in a situation where someone did not understand how you felt about something? You would feel that the lack of understanding had created a barrier between the two of you. It can be difficult to stick with the feelings especially if you are in a hurry. Due to the many demands on your time you may have to move the situation along faster than it would develop naturally. But if this is done along with the client, it may not be felt as a rejection. Since time is such a disturbing factor in crisis this movement will not often be a problem because movement feels much more comfortable than stasis.

The nurse can help the patient and his family to say what they think and feel. This confrontation of feelings can lead to a resolution of difficulties, because so often it is the unspoken that delays resolution. All nurses know about and have experienced this. You will know the anger you have felt when you knew the diagnosis and prognosis of a patient and have been obliged to avoid the whole subject. The sharing and exploring of the feelings associated with the crisis may give greater understanding of their particular response and behaviour. It will help to remove the fear that the individual in crisis is 'going mad'.

It would be a mistake to believe you will solve the individual's problems — only he can do that. You can, however, be instrumental in beginning the process of coping with the crisis. You may set the pattern for a healthy supportive process which helps change to take place. Setting the pattern may involve helping the patient or his family to identify the factors which produced the crisis. Rosemary Johnson (1980) calls these the balancing factors. They are listed as the realistic perception of the event, the emotional supports and the coping mechanisms.

Exploration and clarification of factors in these three areas can open the way to resolution.

The work I have been involved in here in this country and have observed in the USA has been labelled in various ways. Some would call it 'crisis intervention', others would call it 'Crisis Counselling'. Many would regard it as 'Supportive Therapy' or 'Grief Work'. You may stick rigidly to the crisis mode and intervene in Phase Two and not see the crisis abating, but although you may not see any alteration yourself — because of the brevity of your intervention — you may set a pattern. This is the pattern which helps individuals to find the resources to cope.

Some of the responses to crisis, the intervention and expected outcome are illustrated in Figure 1.2. This chart may be more meaningful for nurses who do not find the patient or his relatives fitting into the sequence of events as described by Caplan.

WHY INTERVENE AT ALL?

It could be argued that for thousands of years, millions of people have coped with crisis and mankind has survived. At this very moment, many people in this country are coping with loss or threat of loss. Many more will be coping with an event that causes chaos and disorganisation in their lives. Through the generations this has not produced any damage

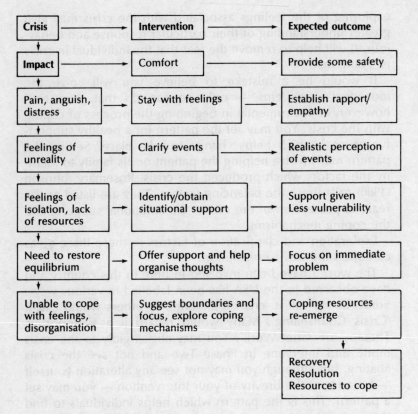

Fig. 1.2 A plan of intervention

which is obviously detrimental to the human race. Despite emotional trauma we have progressed.

If we could just take this global view of life, we could perhaps ignore crisis. Fortunately life has more intimacy than that. We make face-to-face contact with people, their eyes meet ours and we may make physical contact. All of this transmits strong feelings. We may share words which are moving, powerful and disturbing. All of this demands response. We may feel we have this response under control even though the strong needs of all concerned may emerge. In most cases, our humanity will then produce a response, but because we are not devoid of feelings and are not programmed to respond in a certain way, feelings may emerge that surprise, disturb or could even destroy us. We need to come out of this experience in the most beneficial way. Crisis care will help us to do this.

It has been argued by Forer (1963), a psychiatrist, that crisis is inevitable and necessary for personal growth. The suggestion is that this transition period is vital for personal growth and that everyone will benefit from having a crisis.

Murgatroyd & Woolfe (1982) counter this view, pointing out that it is a large step to suggest we should all experience a crisis if we are to be adequately prepared for crisis. Crisis can sometimes enhance our personal growth but the problem is that this is not always the outcome. Risk is a major factor in this hypothesis and we may not only be damaged but could be destroyed. The pain and anguish produced by the disintegration the crisis brings may re-emerge throughout our lives persistently. It may be that the crisis is only inadequately or temporarily resolved. This constant re-emergence of the pain will greatly affect the quality of live thereafter. While a crisis may be good and bad, not to intervene may be too risky.

Murgatroyd & Woolfe also suggest that should helpers fail, the scars will be deep and extensive. These failures constitute a crisis for the helpers in their turn, and the failures and lack of intervention skills have all the ingredients which produce 'burn-out' in nurses.

This possible likelihood of such an outcome begs the question 'Why help at all?' I think the answer is twofold. Firstly, we reduce the possibility of damage by helping people to find coping resources within themselves. By our offering certain skills they are more likely to emerge unscathed or without permanent problems. We thus play some part in increasing the quality of life following some traumatic event.

Secondly we, the nurses, will cope much better with the crisis if we are able to offer something positive. Continuous denial or displacement of painful feelings will eventually take its toll of us emotionally. Crisis care work is very stressful and can become overwhelming. If we fail to respond to the crisis presented to us, the result may be aggression from the patient and his family. As failure to recognise and confront the situation will result in more stress, it is in our own interest to intervene.

Another important aspect of the question is that we cannot fail to respond to the pain and distress of another. It will happen spontaneously and this immediate response speaks more than a thousand words to the recipient. Having begun to reach out in this way we can then continue in a more structured response. This should also enable us to utilize more skills and to gain something more positive from the situation.

Why should the nurse intervene?

This has been answered in part in the previous section. We respond spontaneously to another's need, so let us use this to its fullest extent. Also it has been shown to be in our own personal interest.

Much of the pain and distress in crisis is associated with the medical condition; the course of events of an illness or accident is closely linked to the eventual crisis. The specialist knowledge we have in linking the two is often vital to a patient's or relative's understanding of the whole situation. Our care and interaction with the patient and his family cover every minute of the time we are with them; we will spend intimate moments with the patient, and moments he finds degrading or demoralising. We will have some awareness of his strengths and vulnerabilities. We will have been present in his darkest hours and also in his brightest periods. This is not only a privilege but gives us a great advantage.

We will, hopefully, have created some rapport and empathy which is a good base from which to begin the work of intervention. I firmly believe that patients find difficulty in putting themselves in different 'compartments' according to which particular health professional is involved at that time. It is equally difficult for us to postpone expression of our own feelings while we care for the more obvious organic problems. The illness or accident may require treatment by certain procedures as well as general care, and it is much more comfortable to share the feelings associated with every part of the patient's experience as they occur.

The reality about the question 'Why the nurse?' is that on many occasions we are the only ones around. This applies particularly out of office hours such as evenings and weekends. Crises inevitably occur at these times too, and so to put it bluntly we may have no choice.

If we want to be able to give this more holistic care, albeit without an element of choice, it is surely better that the care be good. To achieve this we need to gain more insight, and therefore more skill, in crisis and intervention.

QUESTIONS FOR DISCUSSION

1. Describe the difference between stress and crisis.
2. Discuss the stages of crisis and how these will change your approaches to intervention.
3. Discuss the statement: Crisis is a useful means of personal growth.

REFERENCES

Caplan E 1964 Principles of preventive psychiatry. Basic Books, New York
Erikson E H 1950 Childhood and society. W W Norton, New York
Forer B 1963 The therapeutic value of crisis. Psychological Reports 13: 275–281
Johnson R 1980 Recognising people in crisis. Nursing Skillbook, Intermed Communications, New York
Murgatroyd S, Woolfe R 1982 Coping with crisis. Harper and Row, London

2

Life transitions

In this chapter we will consider some of life's transitions and how they affect a patient's response to nursing care. We will explore the way in which some developmental or coincidental crises may alter both our approach to the care we nurses give and also how that care is perceived by the patient.

Transitional life crises are for most of us a normal process — some are areas over which we have some control, e.g. getting married is a step which will mean changes in role and status for us. Other transitions will occur because of physiological changes. The first stage of physiological sexual development is prenatal and the second stage is puberty, which brings about anatomical and physiological sexual changes. This transition from childhood to adulthood then takes on other dimensions which are sociological, and include consideration of social, moral, emotional and psychological issues. All these changes in role, together with the individual's response to them within himself, denote the start of adolescence. Although we may have no control over the physiological changes we may be able to have some control over our response to them.

A person's life is composed of inner and outer aspects. The outer aspect concerns our membership of society, our family and social class and our work. This is how we present ourselves to the outside world. For some reason there is often an immediate need to identify us with these areas:

'What does he do?'
'Is he married?'
'Where do they live?'
'Do you know her parents?'

The inner realm is about how we feel about being part of all this. It may be felt to be an advantage or the opposite. Although it may not always be comfortable for us to be part of all that we are identified with, it is at least familiar. Changes away from the familiar may produce a transitional crisis and this will demand something new from us.

It is the disturbances in our inner realm that produce conflict. We may say 'I have felt uneasy and unsettled since we moved house.' This suggests that the external factors have produced change but it is our inner response to them that has produced the unease:

'This is the wrong time to be ill.'
'This is the last thing I need.'
'I can't stay in hospital because my business is in a bad way at the moment.'

There are many occasions when we have a strong suspicion that a patient is under a great emotional pressure. When this occurs it is the patient's inner self we need to work with, i.e. his feelings. Intervention on an emotional level may be offered at different stages of the transition just as help may be needed before, during or after the change.

Gail Sheehy (1977) divided how we feel about our way of living into four areas:

1. Interior sense of self to others.
2. Proportion of danger to safety.
3. Our perception of time. Do we have plenty of it or is time running out?
4. Our sense of aliveness or stagnation.

These same areas can be applied when we are dealing with crisis in hospital patients. Firstly, there can be a time when they fear changes in their interior self due to damaged self-esteem resulting from being a patient. Secondly, many patients feel a very real sense of danger. Thirdly, time often becomes a very important factor with some patients, and on exploring why with them, their areas of vulnerability are often highlighted. The fourth area highlighted — stagnation and aliveness — is particularly pertinent. Loss of vitality and the inability to move forward affect the heart of our most important needs.

These four points serve as a useful guideline in areas affecting the quality of our patients' lives. We will consider how they interact when someone becomes a patient while experiencing one of life's transitions.

INFANCY AND CHILDHOOD

The effects of the separation of infants and children from parents during hospital stays are well documented. Open visiting reduces the feeling of alarm experienced by children, and results in fewer complaints amongst paediatric nurses, who recognise its value. Separation produces not only crisis but also long-term effects on these children.

Schaffer & Callender (1959) studied 75 infants under 12 months of age, who were admitted to hospital. Each child was observed for 2 hours during the first 3 days of hospitalization. The infants, who were without their mothers, had little interaction with the nurses.

The observations showed that the intensity of agitation, fretting and protest was as great in babies of 29 weeks and over as it was in 2- and 3-year-olds. At 28 weeks and under, the symptoms were less intense and the distress less obvious. In babies over 28 weeks, the responsiveness and friendliness were much more marked in response to parents than to nurses. Below this age the babies responded the same to the nurses. This study emphasised the age at which separation can begin to produce distress.

Bowlby (1981a) describes the way this transitional crisis is often manifested as anger. This may be directed towards the parent or the parent substitute and as you, the nurse, may be the parent substitute it may be directed towards you. When you see some of the aggression and hostility directed towards parents you may feel you are witnessing a badly behaved child. Although this may be the case, you should be aware that it could be a behavioural sign of fear of separation and loss. Some children, who are brought to the Emergency Department for treatment for a minor injury, need to be aware from an early stage that they are not being brought for admission. Bowlby discusses the child's response as being the anger of hope or the anger of despair. This describes graphically the responses I have met: some anger from children who are admitted to hospital is an outpouring of anguish and profound loss and misery. The anger of hope is full of argument, persuasion and expectation that the situation can be reversed and the admission prevented.

In his work on attachment Bowlby (1981b) describes the three phases of behaviour in children when hospitalized, and these again describe behavioural changes. They are protest, despair and detachment. It is these behavioural signs that will give us the signal to work with the feelings.

ADOLESCENCE

Adolescence presents many problems for nurses since it can cover a wide age range. Some girls are clearly adolescent in behaviour at the age of 12 and when they are admitted to a children's ward they resent being surrounded by murals of cartoon characters and bunny rabbits because they feel they are grown up. Boys of 16–17 years of age may not want to be examined in the presence of their mother or father. Parents can often be hostile if they are excluded, being very much aware of the child in the patient. They would prefer to be given information first hand as it is often clearer that way. They may be hurt that their 'child' has confidences with the doctor or nurse and not with them, and they may become resentful of the staff.

As much adolescent crisis is concerned with image and bodily changes, hospitals encroach on sensitive territory. It is in adolescence that the 'body image' has to be reappraised. Many of the physical changes of puberty have a sexual meaning. The shape and size of a young woman's hips and breasts will alter the way she views herself, as well as changing how others will see her. Her menarche, sexual drive and developing genitalia have a strong impact on her body image.

Likewise, the young man's adaptation to his deeper voice, sexual drive, erections, penis size and bodily hair will alter his body image. He must leave the familiar and enter the new territory of the adult world with this new body image. He may welcome the change or face it with fear and trepidation.

The problem is that the changes of puberty are not always welcome to the one experiencing them — a young lady may develop excessive weight and a young man clumsiness or the embarrassment of acne.

Whether the adolescent accepts or is comfortable with his or her identity can easily be highlighted in hospital.

Let us begin with the first physical examination. Imagine someone is looking closely at parts of the body you are very anxious about as to the stage of their development. Girls often imagine their breasts are too big or too small. For many male adolescents, the size of the penis is a time-consuming preoccupation. Adolescents will have had many private opportunities to examine and reappraise these parts. When someone walks in blandly, or quickly confronts them, all kinds of messages are perceived. You may well have noticed the sudden hostility after a physical examination has taken place. If not outright hostility, withdrawal of co-operation may occur, with the resulting loss or breakdown of communication.

In her book *Human Sexuality in the Nursing Process*, Elizabeth Lion (1982) lists many misconceptions and questions raised by adolescents about their sexuality. The nurse, by the very nature of her work, will encroach on areas that highlight some of these sexual problems. You must be prepared to help clarify some issues and misconceptions but in a way that does not make the patient feel a fool for not being in posession of that information. It may be the first time the patient has been confronted with the opportunity to clarify such a situation.

Some of these patients will be rude, brash and unco-operative. This behaviour may distract you from the focus of the problem that is uppermost in their minds.

I remember a young man of 15 years who was going for

surgery for an appendicitis. He became very hostile and unco-operative. When he threatened to leave the hospital, his mother was contacted and asked to return to the hospital. This immediately reinforced the fact that he was not adult enough to be approached directly about his behaviour. He was very hostile towards his mother on her arrival but agreed to talk to his older brother. It emerged that the nurse requesting the urine specimen had not left the room while he provided it. He had perceived by her face that she did not think he was very 'well developed'. When he had asked her what would happen if he needed surgery he had been alarmed by her first few words in which she mentioned a preoperative pubic shave.

'Would she do it?'
'If someone touched his penis, what would happen if he got an erection?'
'Would the hair grow again?'

He discussed these things in a jocular way with his brother, who had enough insight to know they were sensitive and major issues for him. When they were discussed and clarified, the young man went on to have surgery and made a good recovery. He discovered from the nurses that these anxieties were not unusual.

If the nurse had been more aware of the stage of this young man's development, she may have responded more sensi-tively. But there is another reason why the nurse may have responded in a way that was not useful — she may have sensed his awareness about his own sexuality and responded by being brash about her own.

In separating ourselves from our families we begin the search for our own identity and have to make choices, many of which will affect our whole lives. To many adolescents it may appear that they have to seek and choose partners, make decisions about work and leading a separate life from their family, all at once. Time takes on an important dimension. Examinations which are taken over a month may have consequences affecting a lifetime. Little wonder, then, that when an adolescent is faced with an illness or accident it can result in total chaos in his or her life.

MARRIAGE

Most people spend the major part of their lives married. The marriage ceremony is the legal and religious pre-requisite to living together and sexual activity. This is changing in the Western world and nowadays, many couples cohabit and regard themselves as 'married'. The crises that occur in marriage are also common to these relationships. Partners may take on traditional roles which are threatened when a partner becomes a 'patient'. It may be necessary on occasions to discuss the value of roles and changes in roles with your patient if the hospitalization produces a crisis (see Table 2.1).

Table 2.1 How illness and accident may alter the traditional marital role

Traditional marital role	How illness/accident may alter this
Male Strong wage earner. Head of the house. Decision maker. Authoritarian father. Arranges social interaction. Active sexual partner.	No income. Loss of leadership. Decisions taken by others. Loss of authority. Loss of control. Loss of social contacts. Reduced sexual activity. Not the same man she married. Change may be needed.
Female Housekeeper. Attractive. Loyal. Supportive. Nourishing. Manager. Nurturing. Uninformed. Submissive. Sacrificial. Passive sexual partner.	No housekeeper. Disorganisation in household. Lack of proper nourishment for family. Mismanaged. No-one to nurture/support. No-one to 'offload' onto. Lack of a totally dedicated person to care for him/them. Non provision of sexual activity — will he look elsewhere?

Often, a mother who becomes a patient may be anxious as to how her husband and children will cope without her. When they do cope, this produces other problems as it can threaten her role and status. For the first time, many patients have the luxury of time to focus on and reappraise relationships. The role of patient can increase the individual's vulnerability. These two factors combined can exacerbate marital or relationship difficulties, which are often verbalized to the nurses because it is an opportunity to disclose confidential information. As most people believe they will not return and see the nurse again, it makes it easier to treat the nurse as a confidante and reveal anxieties to her.

While I do not think that nurses can necessarily undertake marital counselling, they can increase knowledge and awareness about the appropriate agency that can provide help. Some couples will have been in conflict for many years, and the issues that have provoked the breakdown in the relationship can become critical during a hospital stay. You may be able to instigate some useful counselling for them when they leave hospital.

Parallel development

There is still the popular misconception that couples in a relationship will 'grow' together. If this belief is held, separation or illness or accident can take on greater implications. The hospitalization and reasons behind it, or the illness itself, can be seen to interfere with plans that are part of this parallel development. This can take on such enormous implications that a crisis can occur. That thorny old problem of time will usually emerge. If, for example, a baby was planned and timed to arrive after a certain special holiday and/or final examinations, then for some couples this timing is crucial. They will talk of how they planned it all that way as part of their ongoing development.

Some would say that this growth together is impossible and that to try to function within its boundaries will prove disappointing. Husbands/wives can move quickly up and down the economic and social scales; families can be torn loose from home and community because of job demands. It would be difficult because of these and many other factors if the two in the relationship felt they had to develop at comparable rates.

What we may learn, if we stick at the marriage/partnership long enough, is some facility to retain a sense of self while giving to the other. Before we can give and accept real intimacy, we must have a reasonable sense of personal identity. As some patients find hospitalization a depersonalizing experience it may cause them some anxiety in their current relationship. Marriage may postpone work on oneself and one's personal identity. Marriage may mean one has to work at being a spouse and possibly a patient as well.

No two people can possibly co-ordinate all their develop-

mental milestones or crises. The timing of outside opportunities will not be the same. More importantly, we all have
an inner life structure with its own idiosyncrasies. Depending
upon what has gone before, each will alternate between times
of feeling full of hope and great potential and certainty to
times of feeling scared, vulnerable and unfocused. We may
feel we have got life altogether and then it can suddenly feel
fragmented, particularly when we are confronted with a health
problem. Here again is that feeling of its happening 'at the
wrong time' — we feel as if everything is out of our control
and this is perceived as a crisis.

These, then, are some of the aspects surrounding a marital
or personal relationship that have the potential for crisis in
patients.

MIDLIFE CRISIS

Despite all the jokes about it, midlife crisis can be very real.
Much is written about it in the popular magazines but it
remains unclear where midlife is. And I suspect it cannot be
pinned down to a certain age. It is not necessarily about the
menopause but would seem to be more about a reappraisal
or reassessment of one's life and the direction in which one
is going. For most people, the reappraisal occurs without any
conscious decision to do so, but again being hospitalized or
incapacitated for a while can give one the space to allow it to
happen. The patient who cannot sleep, with whom you share
a cup of tea during the night, often discusses this reappraisal
with you.

Midlife crisis, then, seems to be about having arrived somewhere and looking at how one will use one's resources from
now on. Underlying this is perhaps a feeling of having
reached one's peak of achievement and beginning to wind
down. The alternative decision may be to invest one's
energies and life in new and stimulating areas. The latter,
whilst being exciting, can produce fear and panic.

This can also be a period of greater awareness that one will
die some day. One may begin to explore in one's mind what
death will be like and how it will affect others.

'Will they manage without me?'

The feeling that one no longer wants to be competitive may produce some sadness. An awareness that one wants the pace to slow down and to have a quiet life may be agreeable but it may also be seen as a loss. It may also reinforce how disappointed one is with oneself as one did not quite 'make it'.

Illness, injury or accident may confirm one's fear that one has reached one's zenith and one is on the downward slope. It may be just what one wanted to hear when the doctor says:

'You will have to slow down.'
'Take things easy.'

How many patients are waiting for permission to do this. It can offer a way out of the competitive world that is not simply 'opting out'. There are many who will welcome this opening of the way to a reappraisal of pace and direction.

There are others for whom it will spell doom. It will be the beginning of the end. It will not open new vistas, new opportunities. It will slam doors in their faces. It will take away opportunity. They will lose purpose, status and vitality.

For many this midlife crisis is concerned with sexual changes. It is estimated that only 10% of women are inconvenienced by the symptoms of the menopause (Katchadourian & Lunde 1975) and this is said to be because there are volumes of information and more women know what to expect.

Reports about the male menopause and its association with declining sexual activity are less specific. Lionells & Mann (1974) state that most men have enough moderate sexual activity deep into old age. The study by Katchadourian & Lunde revealed that for 85% of men the change is slow and gradual and that most hardly notice it at all, at least not enough to feel it is a problem.

For women the symptoms may be more acute and distressing. Being faced by some other medical problem may again offer the opportunity to confront and clarify this question. Many nurses deny this very special role that they have in preventitive medicine. They may well prevent a crisis; patients, with the help of a nurse, can clarify many issues.

RETIREMENT

Here I will look at planned retirement briefly. Redundancy can be welcomed or can be felt to be as devastating as unemployment which will be considered separately. For some, retirement will be planned, and courses will be taken to encourage new hobbies which will act as a challenge and fill in spaces. Partners will have to spend a much greater part of the day together with all the attendant consequences. Some will have difficulty here, and will use ailments, aches and pains as an escape. Illness may fill a void or avoid a difficult issue. In your nursing history you may hear:

'He's not the same since he retired.'
'He's lost now.'
'He's never had so much illness.'

These clues may indicate some crisis associated with change. Losing the friends of work and the structure that work brings may be painful. The change in lifestyle may have produced a relationship crisis, if partners are unable to adapt to so much time together. Emergency nurses are only too aware that fights between spouses occur even in 60-, 70- and 80-year-olds.

Some of the feelings associated with retirement apply equally well to midlife crisis and unemployment. They will be explored in more detail in the section on unemployment.

DEATH

A whole chapter has been devoted to sudden death because this produces many more problems for the relatives and staff. It is shown in that chapter how studies have demonstrated that the sudden death is more likely to produce a difficult crisis. Any death is painful and confronts us with perplexity, ambivalent feelings and anguish, but if we can anticipate the loss, we may be at an advantage. If we are able to mobilise resources and coping mechanisms beforehand, we may cope with the loss more adequately.

Speck (1978) talks about offering or helping relatives with anticipatory guidance. Realistic information will help people to be aware of how they might respond. This increases their awareness and increases worry. This 'worry work' is also given lots of emphasis in Murgatroyd & Woolfe's *Coping with Crisis* (1982)

The anticipation of the loss produces pain, fear and pessimism and the grief begins. Offers of help will be made before the event and these will be taken up when it occurs. After the sudden death, the bereaved may feel they have been left totally alone and helpless, as if in a wilderness. The assurance of support and help, when offered alongside the anticipation of the loss, enables the relatives to participate actively in the loss and to have some control over how the bereavement is managed, even to sorting out their resources in order to cover the event. This amount of control over this difficult time may help to prevent a crisis which will be damaging and will add more pain and anguish to the loss. Speck goes on to say how a sensitive awareness of the implications of the loss and grief can help the person suffering it to grow from the experience. This can make our anticipatory work a great asset in the care of the dying and in crisis intervention.

The chapter on sudden death will explore in more detail the feelings and responses associated with death. What I think is most important in our intervention is the marked difference in response to anticipated death and sudden death. Our skills and work in these two situations demand a different approach and this difference once again highlights how we can feel we approach the situation created by sudden death. This applies to both parties — the relatives and the nurse.

DIVORCE

More and more people are involved in a divorce; few are untouched by relatives and/or friends having gone through this experience and all its turbulence. Many married people, in desperate, tormented and difficult times, have considered divorce, and so are aware of its destructiveness. You may have heard how some people have emerged fulfilled, or have 'grown' from the experience. Very few talk this way. For most it is full of sadness and pain, and is a significant loss.

As more people divorce, the social disgrace becomes less.

The legal system has also changed with the times and it has become easier for people to obtain a divorce. Divorce used to bring shame upon one's family and stigmatise the children as belonging to a 'broken home'. It brought, and still does bring, much discussion into play as to who is the guilty party. 'Where the blame lies' continues to remain important for many. We have a need to label or categorise the individuals involved, perhaps in order to make the divorce seem more understandable.

Epstein (1975) describes graphically the feelings associated with the actual procedure of the divorce court; how in the court one listens to tales of sexual impropriety, hatred, disaffection, unresponsiveness and vengeance. All this is associated with the person one used to love, the person one's dreams were made of. Epstein describes how one leaves the court humiliated, guilty and bitterly disappointed with oneself, painfully aware of how others are disappointed and angry with one. The overall implication is that one is somehow weak, incapable of sustaining a loving relationship. Self-esteem takes a big fall. The other overwhelming feeling is that one is irreparably damaged.

Having shared these feelings with clients on many occasions I can assure you it is an extremely painful experience. It is not at all surprising, therefore, that this damage can become part of one's whole body, and clients become patients. It is much more acceptable to oneself and others to be a patient, rather than a damaged divorcee.

Dr K. Bolden, a general practitioner, looked at single parent families (1981) and compared them with a control group of 'normal' families. The typical single parent family was a woman in her early 30s with one or two children about 10 years of age. The one parent adult consulted the doctor twice as much as the controls, mainly for respiratory problems. There was no evidence that children were coming to any harm physically or psychologically. Termination of pregnancy was significantly higher in this group. Slightly higher was the level of consultation about gynaecological problems and contraception.

Wilson-Barnett & Fordham, discussing recovery from illness (1982), highlight several pertinent points when divorced people are patients. The most obvious need of a patient is a support system and a freedom from anxiety about being away from home. This produces intense distress in single parents admitted to hospital. If a patient's self concept is that he/she is damaged, how will this affect recovery?

Cohen & Lazarus (1979) discussed the framework for studying patients' adjustment to illness. The patient will need to adapt to the stress of illness by, amongst other things, maintaining emotional equilibrium and a positive self-image: not the attributes of most recently divorced patients.

Our awareness of these feelings and stages experienced by patients who are separated or divorced will, I hope, allow us to work more sensitively in these areas. Some of the problems are much more obvious and at surface level. Not working can mean severe financial hardship. At visiting time the patient not visited by a spouse, especially if they have children, will promote discussion amongst other patients and nurses. Some women will be very conscious of the absence of a man visiting, bringing flowers or chocolates. All this has the potential for crisis in our separated and divorced patients. Some local single parent groups are keen to assist other single parents when they are admitted to hospital. It is worth while being aware of this, because if the admission occurs at night or weekend you may be the only person available to arrange any support. It will not only reduce the length of the patient's stay but also may prevent a crisis.

THE ELDERLY

Some of the strongest feelings I have heard expressed by nurses about relatives have been concerned with the relatives of the elderly. Much is said about the 'dumping' of elderly patients in hospital because relatives are unable to cope with them. It is very easy for hospital staff to get into angry verbal exchanges with these relatives. If you look closely at why this should happen, it is not simply a stance being taken by nurses that families should care for their elderly relatives. It is also because the nurses feel they are being left with intractable medical problems and that the bed will be occupied for a prolonged period of time. They will be unable to find suitable accommodation for the patient.

When you are attempting to resist admission you need to make the reason clear to the relatives. Often it is because it is inappropriate to admit an elderly person into a medical bed for social reasons when there are other more appropriate channels. The hospital may also have difficulty admitting that it can do very little to improve the condition of the patient. We are often reluctant to talk in this way because it reduces our power. If the sole reason given for discharging or refusing to admit is because the patient is the relative's responsibility, a hostile response may be produced. It may also not be the total picture and you are not being honest. One way of expiditing a discharge or refusing an admission is to appeal to someone's guilt feelings.

A confused or bedridden incontinent patient, or a difficult and demanding elderly patient, can produce total disruption in a family. Not only is it physically draining but it can be emotionally demoralising. It can mean social isolation because of commitment or loss of home facilities and estrangement from children or other family members. Some families will block the discharge of a manipulative admission — it can become a battle as to who will win. When we reach these measures, desperate moves will be made and impulsive things done and said. Some families will be driven to the limits. Major decisions may have to be made about housing or job. It can easily become overwhelming for all the parties concerned. We are wrong if we take on the role of the patient's advocate only — the health and disintegration of the whole family can depend upon the outcome.

The whole subject of the problems of health and the elderly and the family has many implications. What we need to do is to be more honest with the patient, the family and ourselves, about our roles and expectations. The impact on the family for their future health and the continued recovery and care of the patient are all interrelated. They must be, and this is an important consideration in our objective evaluation of the whole family.

Some other aspects concerning the elderly patient have been looked at briefly in the section on retirement. The principles about the loss of structure, as emphasised in the unemployed patient, will also apply to the elderly.

The feelings of the elderly patient and her family are now becoming an integral part of their total health care. This is well illustrated in a general practitioner's health care plan for an elderly patient. Gauld (1982) includes the spouse's problems and counselling necessary to deal with those problems in the plan of care for an elderly handicapped patient. This in turn should enhance the care of the patient.

THE UNEMPLOYED PATIENT

Most of you will remember how you made acquaintance with the work ethic quite early in your school career with constant reminders from teachers that you were being prepared for the world of work. As you grew towards adulthood you will have been told often about what happens to idle hands. The work ethic is a powerful part of our culture. As we move towards a more computerized age the work ethic will perhaps become less powerful and it will be more acceptable, and even unavoidable, to have plenty of leisure time.

When you lose your job you lose the status of worker. Some people will have failed to obtain work at all, many will have lost jobs. Just as people have difficulty knowing what to say when confronted by the bereaved, so some unemployed people feel they are avoided for the same reason. The more we are identified with our occupation, the more likely we are to feel the loss. Identity and status add stability and structure to our lives. The loss of this can lead to disorganisation and humiliation.

Kate Maughtin (1983) likens the unemployment experience to bereavement, with its ensuing phases. She describes how after the shock and disbelief one can then turn to the hope that something will turn up. When this fails to materialize, one becomes depressed.

Nowadays being unemployed means one is one of 3 million others so there are many people in the same position, but this knowledge can be of no help at all, just as it may not be of help to the grieving widow to know that there are hundreds of other widows like herself.

Loss of income means a considerable drop in one's living

standards and all the hardship associated with that. The longer the situation goes on, the more difficult it is to achieve recovery. The sense of failure is more easily confirmed; in this situation one has not come up to the expectations of parents or grandparents. The question may well be asked:

'Am I really no good after all?'

With the increase in unemployment and divorce in recent years there has been a marked increase in self-poisoning in Leeds. Dr Froods, a general practitioner, found an increase in the incidence of self poisoning in his study of East Cheshire (1982). The increase was noticeable in males and in the unemployed. Unemployment has serious implications for health.

The experience of being without work is a crisis for many. The transition from one job to another may produce a crisis but most find effective ways of coping. More serious are the reactions of the long-term unemployed who become much more prone to crisis as described by Resnik & Ruben (1975).

As you already know, crisis-prone people are much more likely to end up in your hospital. A study by Cobb & Kasl (1977) on the effects of job loss on physical health demonstrated how there was an increased risk of coronary heart disease. This study also highlighted the increased susceptibility to hypertension and peptic ulcers. Although these illnesses are important and will bring us patients, the phychological effects can be devastating and produce a crisis. The lowering and loss of self-esteem, feelings of inferiority and the lowering of morale can all be damaging.

Some individuals will gain more self-esteem and feel more acceptable if they become a patient. This can add structure to each day and replace that lost with the job. Work provides safety and pace, beginnings and endings to each day, and expectations about living standards. Work helps us to plan things in life, such as frequency of holidays and the pleasure these bring. If we are working we may have less need to be ill, as work gives us status and role in our relationships and contact with the community. The loss of work breaks this contact. It removes structure and the loss of boundaries means we can wander aimlessly and feel lost. It can produce isolation through lack of association with work colleagues, and loss of income may mean cutting back on social activities.

Within the family, the unemployed are no longer able to support themselves financially so they become a burden. They no longer feel of value. This not only has the potential to produce a patient, it will also affect recovery. The illness may be a reflection of the crisis experienced within the family, due to unemployment.

BEING A PATIENT

By looking at these developmental and coincidental crises, and how they can produce patients or delay recovery, we can get a more holistic view of the patient, although some will become patients simply because of illness or accident. Some will enjoy the experience of being in hospital, others will see the role of patient as a threat and this will produce a crisis due to the loss of role and status and identity which we value for the reasons previously discussed. Being a patient can be perceived as a threat physically and be something over which we lose power and control. It suggests we will become subject to other people's control and judgement and we may not trust this in the people we have met so far. The whole scenario can become so threatening we may decide quickly and impulsively to leave it all behind us and escape from it. If panic is produced in the patient and pressure is put upon him to remain in this role, he can become totally overwhelmed. His behaviour and responses become disjointed and disruptive. A crisis can easily result from a person's becoming a patient.

This exploration of the common transitional crises is by no means a comprehensive evaluation of them. On looking briefly at how some of life's crises are perceived and the responses they produce, we will hopefully gain more insight into the stages at which our patients have arrived in their lives. It is important that we explore and are receptive to the feelings which are produced by these life transitions. Once again, our role in preventing further breakdown, and increasing the comfort and well-being of our patients, is reinforced.

Case study

Jean was sent along to hospital by her general practitioner after experiencing pain in her abdomen for 24 hours. When she arrived on the surgical ward, a staff nurse took details of her previous medical history which was unremarkable except for a fractured ankle some years previously. This was sustained while playing hockey for the office team. She is married with two children under 4 years of age and previously worked as a secretary. She had moved to the North of England 2 years before when her husband was promoted to regional sales manager for a local motor components firm. Her family, parents and two brothers were in the South and she bemoaned this fact.

She was asked for her home telephone number and her husband's business number. She made some scathing remarks about it being difficult to contact him at work as he seemed to be at endless conferences and meetings. She asked that they take note of her neighbour's telephone number because the neighbour was looking after the two young children. She wanted to be sure the hospital had a link with them. The nurse recorded this but reminded herself they were both under 5 years.

On examination in the Accident and Emergency Department it was noted that the pain was non-specific and that palpation of the abdomen had become difficult due to the patient's inability to relax. She had also asked her husband to leave the Department, saying he was too busy to be hanging around there.

When the nurse took her blood pressure, temperature, pulse and respiration measurements, she observed again how anxious Jean was. The nurse attempted to find out the cause of the anxiety. She commented on how difficult it was to come into hospital especially with two young children. Jean coolly replied that it was not necessarily like that and that she had nothing to fear. The nurse decided not to pursue this topic, and Jean then asked if this meant she was difficult and her symptoms did not fit into the textbook case. Staff nurse was becoming more wary of Jean's underlying hostility — or was it sarcasm? — and the rest of the essential details were recorded in a matter of fact way, and staff nurse withdrew.

A few minutes later, an enthusiastic and pretty young student nurse arrived to take a mid-stream specimen of urine. Jean felt well enough to obtain this in the ward toilets and the student nurse accompanied her. As they passed the lounge, the nurse explained that afterwards Jean could sit with the other patients and watch television if she wanted. Jean's answer was that she could do that at home.

While the nurse was explaining how to provide the urine specimen, Jean became more impatient. 'Is this really necessary?' she asked. The student nurse emphasised how it could be useful in arriving at a diagnosis. Jean's reply to this was 'Do you mean they don't know?' She was becoming more agitated and asked why doctors, who were only 'bits of kids', had to be given all this responsibility. The nurse explained that the registrar would see her later. Jean returned to her bed sighing deeply and registering her disapproval of the NHS. When both nurses compared notes about Jean's responses and reactions, they realised that Jean had not once complained of any abdominal discomfort or pain.

Jean remained apyrexial and rather restless over the next 24 hours. She had spoken to her neighbour on the telephone several times to check up on the children. She asked if her husband had rung up to ask how she was. She wanted to know who had spoken to him. How often had he rung? The Sister assured her that he had rung but did not know how often. This irritated Jean despite the fact that her husband had visited that afternoon for 20 minutes. Jean was much more vociferous about this with the young student nurse. She felt each call should be recorded so that people knew just who had phoned and when. When the nurse asked if anything particular was worrying Jean, she became angry and said 'Why should it?' She went on to say that a young girl like her would not understand in any case. 'What experience do you have of life?'

Jean's abdominal pain returned. After the registrar had seen her he reported he could find no specific focus for the pain, nor any symptoms that would make the diagnosis clearer. Nevertheless Jean was distressed and agitated. When her husband visited that evening he found Jean in a similar state. It was noted that he was ill at ease and kept his distance from her, and that she spoke to him avoiding eye contact. Hostile words were exchanged between them and Jean's pain returned. Before he left, her husband went to Sister's office. He was angry that the symptoms had not been removed and that the doctors were nowhere near establishing a diagnosis.

Sister told him that no explanation could be given for the pain and that her hunch was that it could be related to some anxiety in Jean's life. She then looked him squarely in the face and asked him if he could throw some light on that. 'Ah well,' he replied, 'I suppose she's told you we're thinking of splitting up.' Sister asked him how long they had been thinking about it. It emerged that someone had recently confirmed Jean's suspicious that her husband was having an affair. She was angry and hurt and alone. There was nobody close to pour it all out to. It would only distress her parents if she rang them. The children were difficult and demanding. Her husband was aware of all this but could offer no positive help in providing a solution.

Sister asked him to call at the ward in the morning. She found Jean wandering in the corridor smoking, and invited her into her office. She told Jean that no explanation had been found for her illness and that it was not at all unusual for someone to present with such symptoms when undergoing an emotional crisis. Sister went on to say that she had sensed Jean's dissatisfaction with everyone being unable to come up with an answer to her pain, and she suggested that perhaps Jean knew where the pain came from.

Jean was much more defensive an angry initially, then suddenly started to weep bitterly. She described how she had to control her anguish and distress about her marital problem because it was affecting the children. The effort and agony of bottling up all these emotions was too much for her. Just when she thought she would totally disintegrate, this terrible pain came on. That was the final straw, and even that could not be resolved.

'How much could one person bear?' She could see no answer. She continued to weep and Sister explained how the pain and not being able to come up with any answers about it could be a reflection of what was happening in her personal life. This was made even worse without the situational support and presence of her family. Jean then announced she needed her Mum and it was decided to send for her.

That night she slept without pain or sedation, although she experienced some initial difficulty in getting off to sleep. The next morning she awoke refreshed and had lost that knotted up feeling inside. The registrar and the Sister discussed with her that the focus of the pain would now move to where it rightly belonged — her marital discord. A pain in the stomach that someone might magic away was much more acceptable than a divorce. The feeling of being stuck with some awful agony and not moving in any direction was totally incapacitating. Medical treatment could not offer her any quick solutions for arriving at the desired outcome, but it was felt that some counselling would help Jean look at directions she could follow. When her husband arrived, they all discussed together how they might look at solutions and find a safe place to share feelings without them being totally destructive.

An appointment was arranged for them both to see a Marriage Guidance counsellor. Jean was now certain that her mother's presence would help remove some of her feelings of isolation.

The whole situation was far from being resolved, but there had been some progress. One of the parties involved felt less likely to disintegrate totally.

Jean could have been sent home with no explanation given for her pain, which was real but these pains have a habit of recurring if no explanation can be found for them.

QUESTIONS FOR DISCUSSION

1a. Discuss how the inner aspects of ourself can clash with the outer aspect of our life.
 b. Explore how this will change our response to illness or accident.
2. How will a mid-life crises:
  a. After our attitude to our work.
  b. Possibly be experienced as a loss.
  c. Interfere with our relationships.
3. Discuss the statements:
  Do we have to have a developmental crisis?
  What does it mean if we don't?

REFERENCES

Bolden K J 1981 The morbidity of single parent families. Update 23:12
Bowlby J 1981a Separation: Attachment and loss, vol 2. Penguin, Harmondsworth
Bowlby J 1981b Separation: Attachment and loss, vol 1. Penguin, Harmondsworth
Cobb S, Kasl S 1977 Termination — the consequences of job loss. United States Department of Health Education and Welfare, Cincinnati, Ohio
Cohen F, Lazarus R 1979 Coping with the stress of illness. In: Stone E C, Cohen F, Alders N E (eds) Health psychology. A handbook. Jossey-Bass, Washington
Epstein J 1975 Divorce — The American experience. Jonathon Cape, London
Froods R A W 1982 Self poisoning in East Cheshire. Update 24(6): 1037–1040
Gauld V 1982 A severely handicapped elderly patient. Update 24:6
Katchadourian H A, Lunde D T 1975 Fundamentals of human sexuality. Holt, Rinehart and Winston, New York
Lion E 1982 Human sexuality in the nursing process. Wiley, New York
Lionells M L, Mann C 1974 Patterns of midlife in transition. Monograph from William Allanson White Institute, New York
Maughtin K 1983 The work famine bereaving millions. Counselling 1:46
Murgatroyd S, Woolfe R 1982 Coping with crisis. Harper & Row, London
Resnik H C P, Ruben H L 1975 Emergency psychological care. Charles Press, New York
Schaffer H R, Callandar W M 1959 Psychological effects of hospitalisation in infancy. Paediatrics 24: 528–539
Sheehy G 1977 Passages. Corgi, London
Speck P 1978 Loss and grief in medicine. Bailliere Tindall, London
Wilson-Barnett J, Fordham R 1982 Recovery from illness. Wiley, Chichester

3

Sudden death

It may appear illogical or inappropriate to consider sudden death at this stage in the book but I believe that when this occurs the implications for both staff and relatives are enormous. Many young and inexperienced nurses will find sudden death a cause for concern: they wonder how they will cope on a practical and emotional level; they worry about how they will break the news to relatives and how they will cope with their response. Sudden death appears to be a particularly difficult crisis for nurses to handle, and the areas of nursing where there is most likelihood of a sudden death, such as Intensive Care and Accident and Emergency, are most stressful. Chapter 9 on Staff Stress will examine this aspect of crisis care more fully.

Sudden deaths are defined as those occurring without warning — the unexpected death. Obvious examples are deaths arising from suicide and accidents. Occasionally patients may appear to be recovering well from surgery, or may attend for investigation, and may suddenly die. When the staff have to break this tragic news to the family they themselves may also be in a state of disequilibrium because of the unexpected event and their sense of involvement and failure.

In the Harvard Bereavement Study and the Harvard Omega

Project Study (Parkes 1975) it was demonstrated that the sudden death was much more difficult to grieve in comparison with other deaths where there was some prior warning that death was imminent. This response is clearly reflected on the nursing staff; many of you will have witnessed the clear recall and obvious distress of nurses when they are discussing events surrounding a sudden death.

It is interesting to note that the first writing on crisis intervention appeared after Lindemann's classic paper entitled 'Symptomatology and management of acute grief', published in 1944, which was the result of his work with a grieved population following the Coconut Grove Fire. This club fire, which occurred in 1942, had a death toll of 474.

The intervention in sudden death cases really becomes crisis intervention. Worden (1983) describes how intervention needs to begin immediately at the scene of the loss. He discusses how this intervention in the hospital will need an aggressive approach as people in a state of numbness cannot always ask for help. He demonstrates the importance of helping the survivor to actualise the loss and the way that viewing the body can facilitate the grief.

Before we look at the different settings in which the nurse will work we should consider the responses with which she will be confronted.

EMOTIONAL RESPONSES TO BE PREPARED FOR

The emotional responses discussed here may be expressed on receipt of the news of sudden death or the possibility of it. They are listed in the order of difficulty that nurses experience in coping with them. This information was obtained by the writer from British and American nurses working in Emergency Departments. From the nine responses to be explored, withdrawal produced the strongest feelings of helplessness, and in many cases panic, on the part of the nurse. Crying, sobbing and weeping were the easiest to respond to and were more readily acceptable. This is not to say that the latter response did not cause some distress to the nurses involved.

Withdrawal

When the bad news is given the relative or the whole family may become inaccessible — they may become mute and refuse, or be unable, to listen. At times the individual makes it perfectly clear that he does not wish to hear any more or to communicate. Other messages may be non-verbal, for example covering up the ears or curling up and going to sleep. Two or three people may wrap themselves around each other; this often happens when children are involved. This withdrawal may be a way of assimilating the information just received, along with all the attendant feelings. If you feel that this is what is happening then it is more acceptable, but if the withdrawal is preceded by strong denial that this is happening to them and it is 'not true' and 'go away', then difficulties arise. Other relatives may panic and suggest that the withdrawn person has been permanently damaged by this crisis and may comment that it has 'sent them mad'.

Although a period of withdrawal may be useful, how long do you allow it to continue? Many nurses find difficulty here because it means they have to sit in silence with someone for long periods of time. Emergency nurses feel more comfortable actually participating in something. A non-verbal response may indicate that you have to try some other way, and this may mean physical contact. Someone who is withdrawn may rebuff this and you are left with nothing to offer (so you think) and this may explain why this particular response is so difficult to cope with.

What you do have to offer in this situation is your presence, which may remain a comfort. You can continue to talk unless specifically asked not to; you can discuss how painful and distressing it all is and how the individual might feel a need to deny what is happening and hope it will go away. You have to make it clear that the problem won't just go away and there are things to work through and sort out. Physical contact may be attempted again.

Unhealthy withdrawal should not be confused with the time people need to find resources within themselves to respond to the information given. Nurses in these situations often describe later how helpless and useless they have felt and how emotionally fragile. They find it difficult to accept the value of supporting someone silently and yet powerfully by their presence.

Denial

The first response from relatives is often 'This cannot be happening' or 'It's not true.' You may be asked several questions to make sure you are talking about the same person. This is a questioning about the fact and/or the reality of the news you have communicated. When overwhelmed by the feelings attached to this sort of news the family or individual may deny the feelings belong to them: 'Tell me I'm not really feeling like this.'

Denial, therefore, can be about the facts, the feelings, or the reality.

We must not under any circumstances collude with this or allow other family members to do so. The response of 'There, there, it will be all right' may seriously affect your relationship with this family when all is far from all right. You can suggest to other family members who are tempted to slip into this role that the outcome can be quite the reverse of all right. Families will value your frankness and honesty with them and admit this to you later.

The difficulty this response gives the nurse is probably caused by her being aware of her own inner conflict in wanting to protect and care for the distressed relative. There is often a moment when you yourself could go along with the denial.

Anger

This may be directed at you, or the doctor, the hospital or the ambulance personnel. If it is directed at the family itself, you may find it easier to cope with. When it is directed at your friends and colleagues it is difficult not to jump in and defend them. You can so easily get caught up in some of the factors which may have prevented something happening. Many nurses have felt in immediate physical danger; it is not unknown for people to kick or punch the wall or furniture. Some families have been estranged for many years because of the hostility which emerged after a sudden death.

Again you are attempting to maintain rapport with the person or family, and to increase empathy. You can so often diffuse the feelings by saying how you understand them, how when you lose the people you love most it makes you want to fight to keep them, how it is all so difficult to believe and understand, and that it is so much easier if you can put all the blame onto one person. Then you are not seen as suppressing their reactions, but as understanding how they are feeling.

Isolation

Despite being surrounded by a loving family and friends a person may express feelings of being totally alone and bereft. Other members of the family may find this particularly disturbing and distressing. They may attempt to convince the person of their continuing support and presence. To tell them at this stage that others will care for and support them may prove difficult and may not be found useful. It moves the bereaved person away from the immediate loss which embraces everything and it is this loss you are confronting now, and this moment in time is what you are working with and sharing.

Bargaining

This response seems to emerge mainly when dealing with the death or imminent death of babies and young children. Parents will suddenly offer to sell all they have in order to put things right or obtain the very best expertise. Husbands and wives will promise each other that they will change their styles of behaviour if it will alter things. They will promise to be good and ask if they have been bad and say they are not knowingly so. Elizabeth Kübler Ross (1973) describes this as 'trying to do a deal with God'.

This bargaining is usually short-lived, and ends when parents regain some insight into the fact that there are some things over which we have no control. You can, of course, state that everyone will do all that is possible despite how much money anyone has. Some remark about how life is of inestimable value to the family may reassure them. If they belong to a minority group they need to be sure they will not be discriminated against, and they must be strongly reassured if they should suggest it as a possibility.

Inappropriate responses

Laughing instead of crying is one of the more obviously inappropriate responses on hearing of a sudden death. Adolescents may respond this way and feel guilty about it later. In a few instances the death of a hated spouse may produce happiness which seems quite appropriate for the individual concerned. Less common are the reactions that surprise and leave the nurse speechless: one example is the young wife who, on being told of her husband's death, said 'Oh dear, we had tickets for the theatre on Saturday!'

The individuals who respond this way are often surprised themselves and may apologise. If they continue to respond in this way it could be that the focus of what has been said is too painful and the feelings that go with it too disturbing, so they prefer to consider some more trivial aspect on the periphery. You may be asked why they respond in such a way. The explanation, when given, moves the focus back and strong feelings may be discharged.

Guilt

As an initial response this is not at all unusual. In the long-term it can produce emotional damage to an untold degree. Most sudden deaths produce some guilt in the family. This is often centred on why they did not recognise signs of illness or why they decided to take a certain course of action that day. I am convinced that many are checking out with the nurse the way others will respond to their part in the event. The question of whether we can ever have total control over all aspects of our lives can be discussed usefully. On occasions you will hear a story recounted where there is strong justification for feeling guilty. Sit and listen to it without being judgemental or denying that the guilt should exist. The very fact of its being shared can have a therapeutic effect.

Crying, sobbing and weeping

This is a more concrete reaction to which you can respond fairly easily. It demands comfort and it feels more comfortable as it seems an appropriate way of reacting. Most nurses have little difficulty here. For others the crying goes on too long and some families will want ways of stopping it. To some people, it will be seen as a sign of weakness — loss of control — whereas in some cases the person may wish that he could start to cry. More people today recognise the value of crying, and some will save this discharging of anguish and pain for more private moments. It disturbs me that there are some who cannot share it with others or have nobody to share it with. Many people will want to cry and will need you to help them focus on the feelings that will help them begin the process. An experience such as viewing the body may help others to begin the process.

Unfinished business

You may have to spend some time listening to regrets about things left unsaid or things they did not get round to doing with the deceased. This is often referred to as unfinished business and may need further exploration at a later date in order to bring this area of conflict to a satisfactory conclusion.

Roberts (1984) listed the most unpopular patients in rank order using a 'likes' scale, which was coded from '1 — Enjoy caring for them very much' to '5 — Dislike caring for them very much'. Caring for the relatives of the terminally ill proved to be more unpopular than the actual care of the patient himself. The same problems occur in the case of sudden death, in that the care of the patient is preferable to the care of the family, because of the response a sudden death produces in that family.

Kelly & May (1982) reviewed the literature on 'Good and bad patients' and suggested an alternative framework using as its starting point an interactionist conception of the nursing role. They also suggest that patients come to be defined as good or bad, not because of anything inherent in them or in their behaviour, but because of the interaction they produce between themselves and the staff.

The interaction resulting from a sudden death is disturbing and distressing for nursing staff. It makes the relatives unpopular to care for because the feelings that confront us demand some response and interaction. Roberts' study (1984) highlights how third year student nurses had a strong dislike of nursing the terminally ill. One of the reasons cited was having to deal with the patient's relatives, and this in turn demonstrates the stress and inadequacy experienced by nurses in these situations.

If we look at some of the responses brought on by a sudden death and try to understand them, we may feel better prepared and less likely to feel suddenly incapacitated.

Nevertheless knowing what to expect in theory will not protect us from being confronted with the power of the feelings. We have to learn by exposure to them. Knowing all this will not enable us to put things right for the family as a matter of course, or to take control of everything. It will, however, help us to feel less impotent and more comfortable with the situation. Equally important is the way in which we can help individuals to feel they are responding as many others do when faced with sudden death, and reassure them that they are not 'going mad'. We can also help people to understand how to begin to grieve in a healthy and useful way.

BREAKING THE 'BAD NEWS'

You have now spent some considerable time with this family or relative. You have seen various feelings expressed, know a little more about them, and they know you better. Though you were complete strangers an hour ago you now know some fairly intimate details about them, how they feel and relate.

If the patient is being resuscitated and things are not going well, you can pass this information on. The medical staff may suggest that resuscitation attempts will be abandoned. You can then tell the family that things look bleak and that the team, despite vigorous efforts, is getting no response. Some people can be usefully prepared in this way; others will believe to the end that things will turn out fine. If the patient is dead immediately resuscitation is abandoned, most families will expect the doctor to tell them this. He must do this with the nurse's support and in her presence as he will be meeting strangers. On some occasions when the doctor has not broken the news, it has emerged that he did not want to see the family as he had something to hide. Although this may not happen often, and nurses could do this job equally well, it is a situation better avoided. If the problem of 'hiding something' is introduced, it may impede the grief process and restoration phase.

After resuscitation attempts have ceased, some patients will continue to breathe and have a cardiac output for a short time. The doctor can then explain that there can be no further useful intervention and the patient will die in a short time. The family can then be given the opportunity to sit with the patient until he dies. The patient should be disconnected from the monitor as some members of the family could concentrate on that and when a cardiac tracing on the monitor goes 'flat' further unwanted panic may result. All intravenous infusion lines and endotracheal tubes should be removed prior to the family's vigil.

There are no special words to use when someone is dead. Junior nurses are often surprised that the word dead or died is used. It sounds blunt and unfeeling. It is far better to say dead or died than to use some other ambiguous phrase that is unclear or misconstrued. Phrases such as 'passed on', 'left us' and 'slipped away' should be avoided for this reason.

Most staff who have to impart news of a death and all its finality will want to make physical contact while doing so. This probably helps them as it helps the recipient of the news.

Many nurses will ask 'But what if I cry?' believing that this shows some weakness or lack of professionalism. On the occasions I have seen this happen it has increased the feelings of caring and understanding.

VIEWING THE BODY

On being told of the death of the patient, the family will usually want to see the body. There may be various reasons that cause them to arrive at this decision. One is that there may still be an air of disbelief and the viewing may confirm something they cannot come to terms within their mind. In the long-term, families often regret they did not see the body. As many sudden deaths require an autopsy it may be more acceptable to view the body at this stage; if relatives suggest that they will view the body in a day or two any such difficulties should be pointed out.

Another reason for relatives visiting the deceased now is to say goodbye and to reaffirm their love of the patient. Many will say that they had to touch or kiss the patient for the last time.

A third and important reason is that this may be the first opportunity to make a positive identification of the deceased. If this is the reason, the viewing may need to take place in the presence of a police officer. If they or you do not wait for that officer, they will be asked to return later and go through the procedure again. This can often add to the distress of the family. You or the officer will need to explain carefully how identification is necessary for legal reasons, in order to satisfy the coroner's office and court. This aspect can often introduce some hostility as it may suggest that someone is being accused of something. Chairs should be placed at the side of the deceased to allow time for sitting and talking or thinking.

When someone has suffered severe multiple injuries and/or facial injuries, the relative should be warned about it. The Emergency Room staff will have made the patient as present-able as possible. They may decide, for example, that one side of the patient is more acceptable to view. In this kind of situ-ation you will need to stay with the members of the family to protect them from unnecessary distress. If this is not a problem, you may withdraw and leave the family alone for a short time, but you should remain easily accessible.

No relative should not be put off from seeing body even if it is disfigured. It is the individual's responsibility and they may not have the opportunity again. Many people express guilt and feel they have failed the deceased in some way by not seeing them. For others, not viewing the body may prolong denial and cause the grief process to take longer.

Equally, pressure should not be placed on anyone to view the body. It should be pointed out that after autopsy they may not wish to, and after the funeral it is not possible. When this has been explained, the responsibility lies with them.

It is not advisable for young children to view deceased patients with disfiguring injuries. If this is not the situation, many children of all ages have visited deceased patients in hospital. In some cultures it is quite natural. I have witnessed young children looking at a brother or sister and heard them say goodbye. But it is important that children are not led to believe that the deceased is only sleeping, as this may provoke sleep disturbance problems when the deceased fails to re-awaken in the future. It may be necessary to use the word dead.

NURSING AREAS WITH SPECIAL NEEDS

On the wards

Caring for the relatives of a sudden death patient is time consuming. Rooms offering privacy and comfort need to be away from the noises and daily bustle of the ward if possible, as both nurses and relatives need freedom from distractions. Nurses are very reluctant to ask the nursing administrator for help in these situations and this can make the event even more stressful for the relatives and the nurse.

A special feature of sudden death is an increased need to understand why it has happened and more details may be demanded. The state of disorganisation produced in the family or individual gives you, the nurse, more work. You may have to spend considerable time seeking out the people that the bereaved want to come and support them and transport them home. It may take lots of patience to elicit the correct information to enable you to carry out this vital task effectively.

Other members of the nursing team, especially junior staff, may need some support in dealing with a sudden death, and many doctors will also feel they want to talk through the attempted resuscitation and how the relatives reacted. Other patients will also ask what happened and be aware of the death. I always found it extremely uncomfortable and embarrassing when nurses returned to a ward after a body had been removed and, on being questioned, refused to make any reference to the death. As we do not disclose confidential information, we must acknowledge the fears of the patients in the ward when one of their number dies.

If ward staff have only limited knowledge of the patient or his family because he has just been admitted, they may feel at a disadvantage. This highlights the importance of identifying 'key' people in the patient's life and ascertaining who is present. The nursing process documentation will help and remind you about this.

Intensive care and coronary care units

These special units, along with others such as special care baby units, add another dimension to sudden death. The machinery, technical equipment and special clothing may contribute to the unreality of the death. Some families cannot even identify loved ones in these surroundings and will ask for confirmation that the deceased is their relative. They may need extra time to help them actualise the loss. Besides assisting them to view the body, it may be necessary to spend extra time discussing with them how they feel, rather than going over the circumstances of the death or who was to blame.

The accident and emergency unit

The reception and management of the patient needing resuscitation demand many responses from the staff, above all a sense of urgency which does not impede or lessen practical skills. Several team members may demand various courses of action and someone will have to exercise some responsibility for leadership to help establish priorities. Routine vital signs will begin to be monitored as clothes are cut off or removed. The urgency and crisis will be apparent and to the uninitiated it may appear chaotic. The situation needs careful management as some members of the team may experience difficulty in controlling their feelings: their inability to deal with the patient's immediate needs may produce feelings of helplessness and hostility.

Ambulance crews who have had sole responsibility for the patient until now will be giving details of the incident which precipitated his admission. They may give a name, an age and an occupation. It may be they know that the patient's wife is on her way to the hospital. The unconscious patient then begins to acquire some identity and we begin to see him in some family or life situation. As the picture of this person builds up, the whole scene has more emotive implications.

While the staff involved in the resuscitation are being stretched, another nurse will be preparing to make contact with his wife. Perhaps this nurse wishes she was facing the demands of the resuscitation room rather than meeting this lady. If the relatives have travelled in the ambulance, they may well have witnessed cardio-pulmonary resuscitation whilst travelling at high speed with sirens blaring. If they did not travel in the ambulance, we cannot be sure until they have seen the patient that he is who we think he is. Is it really this lady's husband? How prepared are we to handle this? We have to meet complete strangers at a dreadful moment in their lives, and care for them. We need to establish rapport with them and be able to communicate information in a way they can understand it.

There are not only some very important practical considerations to look at but some very powerful feelings to handle.

Useful practical points

On notification from ambulance control of the imminent arrival of a patient for resuscitation, a nurse should be allocated to the care of the relatives. This nurse (you) will meet the ambulance to receive any relative or friend who has travelled in it with the patient. If the patient arrives alone, you may be able to obtain details of identity from personal effects and details of the incident from the ambulance staff. Family and friends will want to know quickly what happened. You will then notify reception that any enquiries in person or by telephone must be directed to you personally. Any contact made by telephone from the hospital is made by you. Such contacts will be asked to come to the hospital where 'a person believed to be Mr X has been admitted in a critical condition'. They will be requested to ask for you by name, and also to get someone to accompany them to the Emergency Department. It is important that they understand clearly who you are and where you are speaking from. It will cause severe distress if, after they have put the phone down, they find they are unsure of the location.

A room within the Department, but out of hearing of what is happening, is essential. This room should have comfortable seats and a telephone with access to outside lines. The family may have to spend a long time in this room. Tea- and coffee-making facilities should be available and there should be easy access to toilets. Ideally, the room should be soundproofed to prevent the sounds of the family's distress disturbing others within the vicinity.

When you meet the family, introduce yourself and give brief details of what happened to the patient. This should be done in the privacy of the room. Your words and explanations will be imprinted on the family's minds for a long time. Explain that this is how you understand the situation but you have yet to obtain the details. Explain that your role is to care for them and to keep them informed of what is happening in the re-suscitation room. As soon as it is practicably possible, you will arrange for them to identify the patient positively. An item of clothing may be described or shown to them or some item of the patient's property. For them to have to wait a long time without seeing the patient will cause both them and you much anxiety.

After the initial impact of the news and information they will want to be kept up-to-date. You will then be able to inform resuscitation room staff that you have possible relatives and require the latest information for them. Do not leave anyone alone for long or you may find they have wandered away looking for you. Next, help the family to contact any other person they may wish to have join them.

The doctors in the resuscitation room will require details of significant medical history and current medication. When you explain how important this is, it helps the family to focus and talk about the patient by name. This may be useful to you and the family in the long-term. Prolonged resuscitation and other investigations such as brain scan may mean you spend long periods of time with the patient's relatives. You may then be confronted with various feelings, emotions and responses, some of which may surprise you as well as the person experiencing them and other family members. These responses may cause difficulty for you as nurses are often ill-prepared for them. We will explore this aspect of the subject in more detail later.

Although some of these practical points may appear obvious, it is important that they are stated. If a relative becomes angry and full of revenge, he may later become preoccupied with some practical aspect of the death if it is mismanaged. Loss or bereavement may not be handled usefully and all the feelings may be displaced and focused on this aspect of the incident. It may well interfere with the normal grieving process.

Sudden infant death syndrome (SIDS)

Cot death or SIDS needs separate consideration as it produces some very special immediate needs. Over half the cot deaths in this country are taken to the Accident and Emergency Department as an emergency. For many it will be apparent that the baby is dead, but it is still necessary to try to save its life. The other explanation is that ambulance personnel have a great need to do something positive in this awful situation. Staff should offer the same care as previously discussed but there will be additional and equally difficult dimensions.

SIDS is full of mystery and produces perplexity and a search for answers. Parents may spend a long time examining their care and discussing the absence of symptoms of illness. They will want to convince you that they wanted, cared for and loved the baby. They will often express more guilt and be overdefensive when asked about the baby's health. The involvement of the police may suggest accusations and blame and the police role needs to be discussed carefully. Husbands and wives may be unjustly critical of each other in an attempt to find the answer. It has to be stated clearly that there may not be an explanation, and it is useful if the parents can see a paediatrician at a later date to have this reaffirmed by a specialist in the subject.

An opportunity must be given to the mother to hold her baby when she views the body. As some nurses have difficulty in coping with this emotionally, they may deny the mother the opportunity. This has caused problems for many mothers later, and also has resulted in an extension of their grief period. Husbands and other members of the family may try to prevent the mother holding the baby, but most mothers want to do so and both parents may value time alone with the baby, away from other family members. Remember too that Dad may want an opportunity to hold his baby, and if the baby is very young and they have not had time to have it photographed, then the offer should be made to get this done by the hospital photographer.

Suicide

This is another sudden death which deserves special consideration. Lindemann & Greer (1953) highlighted how the bereaved by suicide tend to feel rejected, and this in turn will produce more guilt and shame. Sadly there remains a stigma attached to suicide which has repercussions on the family. When death is confirmed or occurs shortly after the suicidal act, the nurse may be faced with more anger than in many other sudden deaths. The person who commits suicide leaves the relatives to disentangle his emotional problems as well as to cope with their own loss. This is a heavy burden to bear.

VIEWING THE BODY

As visiting and viewing a body usually take place soon after the death, it is usually done in a part of the Emergency Department. Some hospitals insist it takes place in a chapel attached to the hospital mortuary but this may delay the contact. When it is done within hearing of other nurses, the distress and the conversations with the deceased will disturb many nurses. Staff should be aware of this, and remember that student and pupil nurses and new staff are particularly vulnerable.

It is not unusual for a relative to 'collapse' onto the floor on seeing the body or just afterwards. Be prepared for this and for the panic it produces in other relatives. Most pepole recover quickly. After this period with the deceased, the family should return to the relatives' room. It is not advisable for them to leave the hospital immediately as they will need to regain some equilibrium.

MISCARRIAGES, STILLBIRTHS AND ABORTIONS

Fortunately over the past few years it has been recognised that miscarriages and abortions deserve as much attention and grief work as the previously mentioned sudden deaths. Much more attention is given to photographing the baby in still-births, and going through the rituals to facilitate the grief and recognise the loss.

There are many self-help groups for people experiencing these various kinds of sudden loss, and it is worth while keeping a register of contacts for these groups in your area.

PRIOR TO LEAVING THE HOSPITAL OR YOUR DEPARTMENT

It may now be an hour or more since you first made contact with this relative or family. Many other members of the immediate and extended family may have begun to arrive. You now have individuals who have begun to assimilate what has happened more clearly, but the new arrivals will still be reacting to the immediate impact of the news. You will there-fore be caring for an increase in numbers of people at different stages. For you this stage can be much more demanding because you too have exposed to some very trau-matic feelings for a prolonged period of time. Demands for comfort and directions may increase and you should not feel bad about asking for help.

Practical questions about what to do next are usually asked at this stage. It will be easier for the family if an undertaker is contacted on returning home. He will advise them on such matters as obtaining a death certificate and placing an obituary notice in the newspaper. As the sudden death may need an investigation, the undertaker will inform them about any legal procedures and possible associated delays in arranging the funeral.

Clothing and valuables can be handed to the family at this stage. Clothing should be carefully folded and itemised along with any other possessions such as jewellery and money. You will require permission to dispose of badly damaged clothing and will need to explain why some of it was cut away from the patient. There is often a request that wedding rings and other jewellery are left on the body; this should be noted and a receipt given to the family. Occasionally there is panic later when some item is thought to be missing and the family is unclear about what was said.

Before the relatives leave ask again whether they have any further questions. Give them the opportunity to return to clarify something; repeat your name and write it down for them, so they can talk to you again at a later date if necessary. Many will need to do this; some small aspect of the whole experience may interfere with their thoughts for many months or even years. It is important they take steps to prevent this happening.

No-one should leave the hospital alone as disorientation can be a problem immediately afterwards such as experience. However you cannot prevent this if someone insists. When a patient is transferred to another department in the hospital, such as the intensive therapy unit, the nurse involved in the care of the family should accompany the relative. The details of the psychological care of the family, and of support systems, should be communicated.

These principles of care apply in any nursing where members of a family are faced with the crisis of sudden death.

THE STAFF INVOLVED

Some hospitals will make some provision at this stage so that the resuscitation staff may evaluate how the situation was managed. This is a formal opportunity to examine roles and efficiency and any problems which may have arisen. It also gives staff an opportunity to discharge their feelings about the event. If, for instance, a doctor or nurse was particularly aggressive or abusive, it will give the staff the opportunity to explore why. It is not at all unusual in this highly charged situation for some pretty harsh words to be spoken. Rather than admit to feelings of panic and inadequacy some people will transfer the blame to other more vulnerable team members. This may need pointing out to the individual concerned. If a resuscitation attempt is unsuccessful and all resources were used effectively, it serves as a reminder of our scope and limitations. We may need to make special note of this and not look for scapegoats to explain it away.

If there is no formal machinery to allow for this evaluation and 'time out' for a short period of discussion, we should make one. If we do not, the staff coffee, tea and lunch breaks will be dominated by the subject for a day or two.

Two or three resuscitation attempts following on from one another can be particularly difficult and the staff need some time to regain their equilibrium. The later chapter on staff stress will examine ways of recognising crisis in staff members.

Case study

John was admitted to hospital with multiple injuries from a motor cycle accident. Two of his closest friends travelling home from work witnessed the incident from the upper deck of a bus. They arrived at the hospital before John's father and refused to wait in the room set aside for relatives in the Accident and Emergency Department. They wanted to be sure the police had notified John's father.

John was conscious when he arrived in the resuscitation room but was cold and clammy. He joked about his bike being undamaged as the nurses carefully undressed him and monitored his vital signs. He had a compound fracture of his femur and fractured and displaced bones in his arms. He complained of severe pain in his abdomen and back. While the intravenous lines were being set up blood samples were taken for grouping and cross matching. When it was discovered that he had a tense and distended abdomen, a general surgeon joined the casualty officers and the orthopaedic surgeon. The 'on call' anaesthetist was consulting the neurological observation chart as John joked about how expensive his motor cycle trousers were and how he would sue the hospital for cutting them.

Although he was in pain, John was very concerned about his father and wondered if his father knew where he was. It was explained that he was not at home and John remarked that his father was a workaholic and that was where he would probably be found. This information was relayed to the police.

Plasma was being dripped into John's veins when suddenly without warning, he had a respiratory arrest. He had obviously bled into his abdomen. Cardiac arrest followed as they were opening his abdomen. The many members of the team were coping with their individual tasks as well as the overall problem of deciding priorities. Not surprisingly, voices became fraught and hostile. It was then decided to perform a thoracotomy. Despite all the measures taken to resuscitate John, he died. He was declared dead 60 minutes after his arrival.

After the pronouncement of death most of the resuscitation team members left the room except for one doctor completing documentation and another sewing up the large incisions in the abdomen and chest. The room was a bloody mess and a few nurses remained to prepare for the next patient and replace vital equipment. There was also the arduous task of making John's body presentable.

Shortly after this a message was received by Sister to say that John's father had arrived. She took a staff nurse with her as John's two friends were also present. The doctor who certified the death went along to break the news. John's father asked that the two friends wait outside so that he could speak to the doctor in private. The doctor told him that a young man, believed to be his son from the motor cycle registration number, had been brought in with multiple injuries. He went on to say that despite all measures taken to resuscitate him he had since died. He also explained that it would be necessary to identify him positively. The doctor then left the room.

Sister explained that for legal reasons a police officer would need to be present when he identified his son. 'Let's get on with it then,' was the father's abrupt reply, but Sister explained that the staff were not quite ready and he would have to wait. Staff nurse was very uncomfortable with this man's hostility as it became more apparent. 'He always was a bloody fool,' he suddenly volunteered. Staff nurse quickly replied how brave John had been and how concerned that his father should know. 'What do you know about him?' said the father angrily. 'What do you know about the time I've wasted bringing him up for this to happen.'

Staff nurse could not accept these feelings and told him he

should not feel like that and that there must have been much in their lives that was positive. 'What do you know? You cannot even save his life when he gets here.' Staff nurse tearfully defended the rest of the team and Sister, aware that John's friends were probably overhearing the raised voices from within the room, suggested that the staff nurse went to sit with them.

After sitting in silence for a while John's father asked if John's friends could be sent away. He did not want to see them upset. Sister explained that she realised how upset he was although it appeared that he was just angry. She went on to say how anger and hurt were closely linked. and how he could feel let down by John. He told her at length and in great detail how John's mother had walked out on them when John was 3 years old and what a struggle it had been to bring him up alone. All that investment, all that struggling and teaching John to survive against all odds as he had done, all gone to waste with John going and getting himself killed. It all poured out in a mixture of hostility and deep sadness.

When Sister took him to see his son she was relieved that John's face was clean and fresh looking and the injuries were not too apparent. The policeman left quickly and gave John's dad the chance to say goodbye to him alone. Alone with his son, he wept bitterly. When he left the room he was suddenly confronted by the two friends and he put his arms around them and they all wept together. Then, together they left the hospital.

Sister found staff nurse red-eyed in the staff room. Staff nurse discussed how she should have handled the situation and herself better, and said she felt much wiser. They had a very profitable discussion about what is viewed as appropriate in such circumstances and about how nurses have to recognise when individual needs are being met. Staff nurse said she wished she had been better prepared and Sister smiled. She had heard that many times before.

QUESTIONS FOR DISCUSSION

1. Discuss why two of the responses to sudden death will incapacitate the nurse.

2. Explore the idea that nurses will reflect the feelings experienced by relatives where there is a sudden death.

REFERENCES

Kelly M P, May D 1982 Good and bad patients — a review of the literature and a theoretical critique. Journal of Advanced Nursing 7: 147–156
Kübler-Ross E 1973 On death and dying. Tavistock, London
Lindemann E 1944 Symptomatology and management of acute grief. American Journal of Psychiatry 101: 141–149
Llindemann F, Greer I M 1953 Emotional responses to suicide. Pastoral Psychology 4:9
Parkes C M 1975 Determination of outcome following bereavement. Harvard University Omega Studies 6: 303–323
Roberts D 1984 Popular and unpopular patients. In: Faulkner A (ed) Communication. Recent Advances in Nursing Series. Churchill Livingstone, Edinburgh
Wordon J W 1983 Grief counselling and grief therapy. Tavistock, London

4

Distorted body image

Although her condition was benign and treatable, Mrs Proops was still very worried that something more serious might be discovered during surgery.

> Despite all those other ops, my head has always been very good. I've always been very together. But I suddenly came apart with the breast. It wasn't the same as when I lost my uterus. Then I felt somewhat relieved. I thought 'Thank God I won't have all that any more.' But breasts are fundamental to a woman. They represent life itself.
>
> Though I was assured it was most unlikely I had cancer, it had a dreadful psychological effect. The doctor told me there was a 5% chance of its being malignant. I said 'That means there's a 95% chance of its not being malignant.' The doctor was pleased with my attitude.
>
> But it was all a front. I was actually terrified. One of the awful things about a breast problem is the loneliness. I felt totally alone.

This was how Marjorie Proops, the well-known agony aunt and columnist, described her feelings (Campbell 1984). The fear and isolation she describes are common responses to actual or impending changes in body image.

Body image means much more than what we think we look like. It includes the way we perceive our strengths and weaknesses. It must also include the way we perceive our sexuality. It is an integral part of our personal belief system, our hopes and aspirations, how others feel about us and about the way we feel about ourselves. All these things together shape the way we regard our body image, and alterations to this image can be so threatening that a crisis is precipitated.

As babies, we grow and learn to distinguish between ourselves and our surroundings. We become separate from our parents and gain control over our bodily functions. Before all this happens we have no image of ourselves at all. As we grow, the way we look and our image of ourselves change quite quickly. The transition from childhood to adolescence produces many changes. Much of our time at this stage is taken up with how we look. The feelings associated with this can be pleasurable or very frightening. By the time we reach the stage called adulthood what we think about ourselves is intimately associated with our body image.

Any change in appearance or function of any part of our body threatens our body image. This can become a serious threat to our very person, because of the close association with image, feelings, inner beliefs and personal goals. This change does not have to be obvious scarring or disfigurement. For some people, a sudden increase or loss of weight is as devastating as the loss of a limb. Some individuals experience terrible embarrassment because they have to wear a bandage or dressing, or a plaster of Paris. If focuses attention on the body, and can focus on areas they would prefer to remain insignificant. Alternatively it can be seen to contain an underlying message that they are stupied or incompetent.

What we adorn the body with can also be an integral part of that body image. Some of you will have witnessed the distress occurring in some patients when a ring or necklace has had to be removed. Another regular occurance for nurses on surgical areas will be to ask patients to remove dentures prior to anaesthesia. For many, this causes acute embarrassment as they feel their appearance is grossly altered. Many will say how old it makes them look and feel. This, of course, can then increase their feelings of vulnerability which may already be great.

Expressing concern and anxiety about body image can be useful. It is a way of exploring with another person the overall implications of the change. For many patients, this outward expression is both necessary and healthy. The nurse can use

the occasion to affirm that the patient continues to be acceptable and that she continues to recognise him as a person.
Some behaviour may indicate a movement towards a crisis
associated with bodily image. Look for the following signs:

PASSIVITY

This may be part of a change in mood or affect. A lowering
of morale and self-esteem can lead to sadness and withdrawal,
which in turn may result in the patient's not wishing to be
involved in his own care. He may feel that he is unacceptable.
This can lead to a poorly motivated individual as he loses drive
and initiative.

DENIAL

This may be evident by the patient's refusing to touch or look
at an altered part — perhaps a stoma or an operation scar or
damaged tissue. In the case of an amputated limb or breast
the patient may deny its absence. This distortion of the reality
is a strong sign that the patient's equilibrium is in danger.
Disassociation from changes in body image can be very
stressful to the staff. This is because when they try to return
to where the real focus lies, painful associations are inflicted
on the patient. As many patients will resist, there will be the
real fear that the nurse-patient relationship will be in
jeopardy.

REASSURANCE

Persistently seeking attention from staff may be the patient's
way of checking out that he remains acceptable. Self-
denigrating remarks such as 'Nobody really fancied me,
anyway' may be a way of gaining reassurance that he remains
acceptable. A compliment can be very powerful in these situations. It affirms that appearance or image does not detract
from the attractiveness of the total person.

ISOLATION

Isolation may be self-imposed because the patient feels unacceptable. Rather than risk rejection it may be safer to protect himself from it. He may verbalize that he is less acceptable to family and friends. The easiest response of all would be to say it was all in his imagination. The reality is that it is not at all unusual for some family and friends to reject a patient because of changes in body image. You may hear them say:

'He is not the same person.'
'It has totally altered his personality.'

This may be true, but it could also be that they themselves are unable to cope with the patient's visual changes. This, together with changes in the patient's emotional state may cause them to reject him. The family may need help with the way they feel, and the patient may need to discuss it. It is naturally a very difficult problem to focus on. Avoidance of the problem over a long period of time could be too much to cope with, because it would mean controlling or internalising some very strong feelings. The result could be a trigger releasing them all in a very disruptive and destructive manner.

HOSTILITY

Feelings of anger and hostility emerge persistently where patients have a strong awareness of altered or damaged body image. When directed towards you, the nurse, they can be demoralising and difficult to cope with. These feelings may be a protest against the medical profession being 'offloaded' in your direction. The patient may have decided that the establishment and/or staff are responsible for the disfigurement. When this is felt, the integrity and the judgement of the doctor may be questioned. Some patients who have had cosmetic surgery, for example, may never be satisfied with the end result. I know of one lady who had plastic surgery on her nose and felt that her appearance should have shown a very marked change. She telephoned the doctor and hospital persistently to make her point. Her expectations of surgery were totally unrealistic, and one wonders what she was told, if anything, prior to surgery. Her hostility and disruption were very difficult over a long period of time.

Some patients will see changes in outward appearance as being the answer to all their problems. Rebellious behaviour or a provocative response may be a protest about what has been perpetrated upon the person.

If you think about the response just outlined, it may occur to you that we have discussed them in more detail when considering the responses to sudden death. Denial, passivity reassurance, isolation and hostility will all be experienced in sudden loss, and it may be useful when sharing fears about distorted body image to think of the problem in terms of loss, because although there is much more to it than this, loss is a very important component of distorted body image. This is much more obvious in the case of amputations and removal of body organs, but Parkes (1975) compared the response to the loss of a limb with that to the loss of a spouse. His study clearly demonstrated that the grief experienced in both situations can be comparable. Other surgical interventions where visible mutilation is involved, such as mastectomy, again produce a similar marked response to the loss. In this case the loss takes on more than one dimension — not only is there the loss of an organ but also a loss of feminity. Speck (1978) discusses how patients need to be prepared for this loss but will nevertheless need to experience it.

PHANTOM LIMB

Not all denial has psychological origins. In the case of phantom limb there is a physiological explanation. When a patient has had a recent limb amputation, he may experience pain or itching in the limb, or feel that the limb is still attached to him. This does not necessarily indicate a state of denial. Severed nerve endings continue to send messages that appear to come from the severed limb. Until the nerves heal fully, the patient will continue to experience what appear to be irrational sensations. He knows the limb is missing but the nervous system sends him the message that it is still present.

A warning that this will happen will reassure him that he is not losing his sanity when he experiences it.

Inflammation and irritation of the amputation site will cause or exacerbate the phantom limb problem. Any measures you can take to prevent this happening will help to remove these distressing symptoms.

Much of the work on distorted body image concentrates on surgical intervention and on areas which have an obvious connection with image, sexuality and self-esteem. We shall look at these first and discuss management common to them all.

HYSTERECTOMY

For the younger woman, loss of a reproductive function poses a special threat to self-image. Otherwise, much depends on age, social background, marital status and indications for the removal of the organ. Although some will be reassured that the indication for surgery may be one of many, lots of women will have the underlying anxiety that they have cancer. It appears to me that until the laboratory report confirms or refutes this, any other counselling work will often be post-poned by the nurse. This work on loss, the change felt in role as a woman and a mother, and her fears about loss of sexual function are areas to explore.

Quinn (1984) suggests that work on giving information about anatomy and expected outcome should also begin immediately. One study (Abrahams 1983) highlighted how, in a group of Australian clerical workers, 10% failed to indicate that the vagina had an orifice separate from the urethra or anus. In this same study it was also demonstrated that of workers aged between 16 and 35 only 50% could indicate on a diagram the correct location for a tampon. This suggests that some of the work prior to counselling should be to give the patient information.

On television, I heard a gynaecologist discussing hysterectomy, saying how he preferred to carry out this procedure per vaginam. It would appear that if the changes are only internal and there is no abdominal scar, the results are less distressing. Despite this, certain parts are endowed with more emotional significance than others.

Richards (1973) showed that 55% of women operated on under the age of 40 years experienced postoperative depression. The fact that her reproductive life is over and that she can no longer become pregnant is a real mile-stone in a woman's life. For some this may be a relief but it is also a change in role and for some it indicates they are on the path to being elderly. If there has been marital disharmony, it can become the focus for that too, especially if there have been sexual problems. The older woman should not be ignored in this area of sexuality. As Kinsey et al (1953) reported, 80% of women over the age of 60 years had intercourse at least once every 2 weeks. Although it may cause some difficulty to raise this issue with an older woman, it would be denying her sexuality not to do so.

MASTECTOMY

The breast is an integral part of a woman's sexuality and her image. The loss of the breast is mutilating and damaging and may produce feelings of being violated. It will affect the woman's concept of herself, the way she functions sexually, and it cannot fail to affect sexual relationships. When pain and discomfort have been experienced for some time, surgery may be seen as a necessary solution, but this is not the case for most women with a lump in the breast, although they may well accept the need to act quickly once the lump is defected. Problems arise because the surgery does not come at the end of a long road of unsuccessful treatments but is suddenly thrust upon the patient.

How long these feelings last will vary considerably and will again be related to the stability and intimacy of the relationship prior to surgery. Lion (1982), in her study relating sexuality and surgery, again emphasises the need for preoperative and postoperative counselling. This must include the husband or partner.

However, we are not dealing only with the grief for (loss of) a very special part of the body. If malignancy is the cause, the long-term implications have to be considered as well. Schonfield's study (1972) showed that 30–40% of post-mastectomy patients show a psychiatric morbidity.

OSTOMIES

The ostomies which involve the relocation of a body orifice are colostomy, ileostomy and ileal conduit. Here the patient is faced with an obvious change in outward appearance. Attention is focused excretory function which is normally considered a private matter, and may result in the re-emergence of childhood conflicts concerning elimination. Questions that will be asked are:

'Do I smell?'
'Can I still have sex?'
'Am I still attractive?'

Similar feelings associated with other types of surgery will also apply here. An additional problem for males is that the extensive abdominal and perineal surgery may cause nerve damage and result in impotence. Urinary diversion may produce orgasmic dysfunction such as retarded ejaculation. No amount of counselling can put this right, but even though we cannot alter it we should not avoid talking about it.

How we respond

As hysterectomy, mastectomy and ostomies involve radical surgery and therefore are felt to be mutilating as well as having special sexual significance, we must tread carefully with our responses. When dealing with a patient, consideration must be given to the following:

1. The external changes will be those which the patient finds most distressing and you will need to focus on these first.
2. Internal changes, although less distressing, can concern organs of special significance, especially those associated with sexuality, role and reproduction.
3. Previous areas of vulnerability in a relationship may become very significant. You may have difficulty keeping within the boundaries and working with what is happening to the patient right now.
4. The loss of self-esteem, role and strong sexual identity may fill the patient with fear as to how relationships will be resumed.

5. The prognosis and implications of associated malignancy may need to be confronted before some of the previous issues can be discussed. If not, discussion may be needed after the preceeding issues have been covered.
6. Anticipatory guidance preoperatively may prevent a crisis response, especially if it takes the form of exploring the process of grief and other expected responses.
7. Develop the idea that the patient has resources and strengths within himself which need to be exploited.
8. Touch the affected parts and encourage the patient to do this.
9. Try to involve the partner. Encourage discussion of loss with the partner, and also the expressions of feeling which the loss brings out.
10. Do not try to pack in too much counselling at once. As well as coming to terms with the psychological adjustment to loss, the patient is coping with the after-effects of surgery and trying to resume the ordinary activities of daily living.

CANCER

I choose the word cancer rather than malignant disease because it has so many implications for people. The word conveys pain, disfigurement, weakness and death. For most people it contains powerful messages about distorted body image.

Those of us who have access to statistics and other sources of information can be enlightened usefully. Some cancers, for example skin cancers, do not require major surgery, and are not associated with side-effect or serious emotional upheaval. Half of the patients operated on for lung cancer are cured. But only one-quarter of all new patients with lung cancer are referred for surgery. Statistics can be used to say exactly what you want them to say.

An additional problem for the cancer patient is that the treatment may result in permanent loss of fertility. Although this is necessary for the eradication of the cancer or the prolonging of life, loss of fertility can be overwhelming. Naysmith et al (1983) discuss how chemotherapy results more regularly in sterility than does radiotherapy alone, and that men become infertile more often than women after the same treatment. For the younger man, this has special implications about his body image. Naysmith et al go on to discuss how these patients require special counselling and they explore the possibility of making use of a sperm bank if the patient has not completed his family.

The authors also raise the issue of how the image of the patient quickly shifts to one of invalid. This becomes a problem when the patient is cured, because of the difficulty in readjusting to being fit. Imagine if you were faced with a terrifying and life-threatening illness while still relatively young — you would find it very difficult to retain a belief in the future, or perhaps you would feel you were tempting providence if you were to see your image again as one of being fit and well. Some patients will discuss how this change back is full of risk, and many will make the adjustment with fear and trepidation.

Penson (1984) describes how, in cancer, the crisis about distorted body image is experienced equally by relatives. One woman described how she was afraid to touch her husband's body because she was afraid of hurting him. Another described how, every day after visiting her husband, she had to answer telephone enquiries about his progress. Usually she commented that he looked no better and then felt she had to take on the role of comforting the caller!

Some of you will have witnessed behaviour in relatives which appears out of character, as they witness the bodily destruction of the patient. They become over-critical of care given to the patient, or they may want to spend long periods of time with you, the nurse, or talking to other patients or their relatives. Any of this behaviour may be a signal that they are finding it increasingly difficult to cope with the changes in the patient. At this stage, intervention is particularly valued, and is useful in preventing a crisis. Relatives who cope well with this distressing illness will obviously have a favourable effect on the well-being of the patient.

Pearson (1984) reported that nurses need to shift the focus away from the purely biological crisis to a stronger, positive approach to rehabilitation. During a visit to a rehabilitation centre in New York Pearson observed that after 48 hours, the patient begins to worry less about his physical condition and starts to be concerned about reconstructing his life. If the acute phase of the illness is over, the patient may be moved to the far end of the ward to recuperate to make way for new admissions who require more involved nursing supervision. This move down the ward may coincide with the patient's realisation that the bodily changes will not allow him to continue his way of life in exactly the same way as before, and make him consider how many aspects of his life will have to change. We need to be sensitive to the fact that this is crucial time during the recovery process and it, can 'trigger' off an emotional crisis.

REMEMBER HIM AS HE WAS

One phrase which I have heard on many occasions disturbs me for various reasons which are worth exploring. After someone has died, you may recall inviting the loved ones to spend some time with the deceased patient. A common response it 'No thankyou, I'd rather remember him as he was.' This seems a strange thing to say as they may have seen the person perhaps only half an hour before. It is often said when someone has died of a chronic illness or cancer, and there have been gross bodily changes. This response appears more appropriate in the case of a sudden death following injury. I accept that it may be the response of people who have difficulty in looking at someone who is dead or who are wanting to deny the death, but I do not think this is always the reason.

Many people will have great difficulty coping with the physical changes in the patient and will find them very distressing. When the patient has found himself unacceptable, the relatives may respond with 'He would have wanted me to remember him as he was.' To me this response is, in some ways, even worse, because it suggests that we, the nurses, have failed to transcend a barrier and give affirmation to the person in this body. Although the death or loss is sad, if this response is caused by our visual perception of the patient, it is even sadder. When communicating with a patient about his illness, it is difficult not to focus on the physical changes, problems and symptoms. To value and recognise the person within this body, along with his feelings, hopes and aspirations, must surely shift the emphasis to encompass the whole person. My feeling is that this change of focus reduces the possibility of a crisis about body image, especially in cancer where gross changes are seen and experienced.

CHRONIC MEDICAL ILLNESS

Altered body image can be the result of surgery, but many more of our patients experience insidious changes over the years, which distort the body and grossly disable them. Rheumatoid arthritis, asthma and other respiratory diseases may deform the patient; problems may cause the patient physically to shrink in size. In chronic respiratory disease, the shape of the chest and shoulders may change. Think about these changes, and the idea that our physical self is an essential element of our personality and the way we project ourselves. If we shrink physically, what happens to our feelings concerning our status, strength and self-esteem?

There are other bodily changes produced by illness, where I feel we should try to correlate the changes both physically and emotionally. If this relationship between the two is recognised, the denial of disruptive feelings produced by the illness will be averted.

Cultural aspects of body image, resulting in patients' attempts to prevent ageing or to alter body image may well produce illness or injury, or may result in surgery. Plastic surgery comes to mind immediately. As we discussed in Chapter 1, our judgement is impaired when we are in a crisis and it is hoped that this is recognised when a patient makes a decision about plastic surgery. Realistic expectations about the outcome are explored prior to plastic surgery, but, as nurses, you will nevertheless be asked for your advice on the subject. It is worthwhile asking whether some of the changes being considered stem from the relationship the patient has with him|herself, because for too many people their own strength depends upon the image they convey to others.

DIET

You may have encountered people who are preoccupied with diet — nowadays, it would be unusual if you have not. Some of the preoccupation is healthy, but you may have witnessed two extremes:

Overeating

The person who has a low self-esteem, or gets little gratification, may overeat and consequently be overweight. If the change in eating habits is sudden, it may be the result of a crisis where the individual is unable to focus on the real problem. The gratification obtained from this response may be displaced fear and anxiety — either chronic or actue. As obesity has health implications it may be a problem you are confronted with — you may see this behaviour as a reaction to serious or sudden illness. The resulting change in body image will only increase the negative feelings the patient has about himself.

It will be seen, therefore, that crisis can lead to altered body image in some circumstances, and that altered body image can also precipitate crisis.

Anorexia

From both the media and from companies promoting slimming aids, there is a great deal of pressure on women, especially, to remain slim. Some of the pressure is exerted because being slim is healthy, but much of the promotion includes fashion and being sexually attractive and more acceptable. The underlying message received by teenage girls, when diet becomes a problem, is that unless they remain slim and sylph-like, they will be rejected. Another theory about anorexia nervosa is that by rejecting food they interfere with the normal menstrual cycle. This removes the positive reinforcement that they are adult and have a sexual role in life. There is no doubt that several of the female anorexia nervosa patients I have known have been unhappy with the transition from adolescence to adulthood, because of the bodily changes it produced. This was by no means the whole story, but a crisis was produced by the transition. If the crisis was not confronted, or the focus difficult to isolate, long-term eating problems were produced.

Those of you who have seen the thin and emaciated body of the patient suffering from anorexia nervosa will recall the lengths that she will go to in order to alter her body. Of course, the way she perceives herself will remind you of the extent to which her judgement is impaired. Anorexia nervosa is not an exclusively female problem, although in males the incidence is much lower.

Case study

John had very powerful ambivalent feelings about his mother and the control she had over him. On the one hand he wanted to be independent and on the other hand he wanted to be nurtured and loved. He was very angry and resentful at the strength of feelings that his mother produced in him. He suddenly stopped eating but would secretly gorge large quantities of food. He was acutely aware of and embarrassed by the changes in his body brought on by puberty, especially blushing and bodily hair. He felt that by remaining in a cool temperature he reduced the possibility of 'going red'. His need to control the room temperature at home, and his refusal to eat meals, became very disruptive to the household. So great was the disruption that he was admitted to a psychiatric hospital.

This rejection by the family, and his subsequent welcome home, produced more problems. He rarely went outside because he felt very clumsy and strange looking, and conspicuous. His thinness from refusal of food, and his insistance on reducing the room temperature, gave him a lot of control over the family. He had a strong need for his mother but constantly worried in case he was considered a 'mummy's boy'. It appeared that she was resistant to his need for independence and individuality, but responded to his sick role.

When I saw him he was totally preoccupied with his image. After several weeks of counselling, when he was safer with confrontation and was sharing many negative feelings, he asked some questions about his image:

'Do you think my lips are too big?'
'Are my legs too thin?'
'What will girls think about my hairy legs?'
'Do you think my smile looks false?'

With difficulty we were able to move the focus of his problems to his emotional vulnerability and his fear of rejection. Many hours were spend discussing why he had arrived at this stage. At times this felt like an academic exercise but it was one he persisted with. He admitted anxiety about his adolescence, about the fact he would need to function sexually with another person and that this would eventually lead to his leaving home. He felt that to have revealed all this at home would have been impossible as discussions of a sexual nature were taboo. To discuss his fear of leaving his parents was too risky as his mother would have responded by smothering him with love and by taking control of him. His great fear was that he would enjoy this and would remain under her control.

His bodily changes and image became his total preoccupation. He spent hours in front of the mirror looking at himself and changing his clothes and hair-style. His illness wasted 2 years of his life, which resulted in his missing school. Much time was spent affirming that the inner person was of value and acceptable, and that he, the individual, came through any image he tried to present. Many strong feelings emerged about his pain and frustration at feeling different.

He eventually re-emerged when he wanted to catch up on 'O' levels and 'A' levels, and to socialise more. This was fraught with many difficulties and fears of rejection. His re-emergence into society occurred when he discovered his individual potential and was less controlled by peer group norms. He did not feel comfortable having to project a macho image as some of his friends did, and he developed his own taste and style in clothes. It took a lot of courage and counselling to shift the focus from his bodily image to where the real core of crisis, and later anxiety, lay.

John saw his doctor on many occasions. At one stage lumbar sympathectomy was considered for his poor circulation to his hands, which he felt prevented normal social interactions. It is readily seen that his preoccupation with his body image had strong health care implications.

My feeling is that an unresolved crisis precipitated a prolonged period of disability. There were several minor crises during the long period of time in which I counselled this young man. We did not allow them to be displaced but dealt with them as they arose. It was difficult to confront John as to where his real vulnerability lay, and I had to persist with this and resist his shifting the problem back to his distorted body image. He eventually allowed me to expose his fears and anxieties about the transition from adolescence to adulthood. A long time was devoted to giving information about how we function sexually, and what is expected of us. Some time was spent looking at social skills. This was a marked shift for John, away from his conviction that the problem lay with his physical appearance.

The idea that our physical self is an essential element of our personality is not new. Somatic theories of personality can be traced back to Hippocrates. Self-assessment of our bodies can cause reactions in our feelings and behaviour patterns that cannot be separated from our treatment when we are ill. Making patients aware of their body image will be an integral part of your nursing care of more patients, and for others the confrontation of their body image will enable patients themselves to come to terms with the real problem they are facing.

The crisis, which may result if we fail to intervene, may postpone healing and the movement towards recovery.

QUESTIONS FOR DISCUSSION

1. Discuss the phychological problems associated with ostomies.
2. Discuss the response from relatives:
   'I want to remember him as he was.'
3. Explore how preoccupation with diet can be unhealthy.

REFERENCES

Abrahams S F 1983 The challenges of adolescence. In: Dennerstein L, Burrows G D (eds) Handbook of psychosomatic obstetrics and Gynaecology. Elsevier Biomedical Press, Melbourne

Campbell C 1984 Anguish of an agony aunt. Nursing Mirror 158 (May 2) (18)

Kinsey A C 1953 Sexual behaviour in the human female. Saunders, Philadelphia

Lion E M 1982 Human sexuality in the nursing process. Wiley, New York

Naysmith A, Hinton J M, Meredith R, Marks M D, Berry R J 1983 Surviving malignant disease — psychological and family aspects. British Journal of Hospital Medicine 28:7

Parkes C M 1975 Psycho-social transitions. British Journal of Psychiatry 127: 204–210

Pearson A 1984 A centre for nursing. Nursing Times 80:26

Penson J 1984 Helping relatives cope in cancer. Nursing Times 80:15

Quinn M 1984 Facts, fallacies and feminity. Nursing Mirror 159:1

Richards D H 1973 Depression after hysterectomy. Lancet ii:430

Schonfield J 1972 Post mastectomy patients. Journal of Psychosomatic Research 16:41

Speck P 1978 Loss and grief in medicine. Bailliere Tindall, London

5

Self-poisoning and deliberate self-harm

Suicide attempts may arouse feelings of anxiety, anger or hostility on the part of the patient, his family or friends. They may affect feelings, relationships and responses, not only of those directly involved but also of ourselves when we are allocated to a patient who has attempted suicide. As we may experience these feelings, it is important for us to have an awareness of ourselves. We need to explore our own feelings about life and death and attitudes to suicide, and then we can work with the patient objectively and effectively.

In this chapter, we will consider ways to be objective and effective, and will discuss why the care of these patients produces such strong feelings in the nursing staff.

Roberts' study of patients that nurses particularly dislike (1984) puts the second most unpopular patient as the one admitted with a diagnosis of self-poisoning. When Roberts looked at traits that nurses disliked in patients in more detail, he listed 'those who do not help themselves and are able to do so.' Self-poisoning and deliberate self-harm patients are often thought to be in this category because these responses to stress are thought to be in-appropriate. The list of dislikes included aggression, patients who treat the hospital like a hotel, and psychosocial problems, all of which can be applied to the patient admitted with self-poisoning because of the way he responds to stress.

If mental illness appears to be the problem, it is more likely that the patient will be considered lacking in judgement and having poor insight. But if he is simply thought to be a weak character he is more likely to be disliked.

This judgemental response from nursing staff is difficult to change. Some of it is based on assumptions and some on bad experiences which affect judgement. When I asked a group of nurses to recall patient, who had taken an overdose, they all brought to mind an aggressive or 'repeated' attender. To test out the assumptions of nursing staff in our Accident and Emergency Department I conducted a study (1979) on self-poisoning patients. None of us failed to be enlightened about some aspect of incidence: age, sex, busiest times or drugs ingested. All of these patients were referred for psychiatric assessment, and only 35% of patients in the study were diagnosed as being mentally ill.

The school of thought that regards attempted suicide as the result of unhapiness rather than mental illness owes much of its reasoning to Durkheim (1975). His work shows that people with inadequate or inappropriate personalities are caught up in circumstances that make them profoundly unhappy. Being unwilling to tolerate this over a long period of time, they resort to suicide. There are a number of people who experience some sudden change to which they could adapt if they gave themselves time. Instead they resort to suicide on impulse, being overwhelmed by the immediate disorganisation and disruption. Such people are overcome by powerful emotions but they are not ill in any other sense and certainly not in a way that need bring them within the realms of psychiatry. Durkheim pointed out that suicide is more common among the sane than the insane. His school of thought implies a belief that psychiatry can do little to prevent suicide insofar as psychiatry is used to treat people for mental illness.

The other school of thought believes that most of those who commit suicide are mentally ill, i.e. they are suffering from a definable mental illness such as schizophrenia or depression. In the mid 1960s when I began my training, many people were detained under the Mental Health Act for taking an overdose of drugs. Of the 1500 patients coming through our Department in 1983 with self-poisoning, only 10 were detained under the Mental Health Act because of suicidal behaviour associated with mental illness.

It would appear that today more responsibility is given back to the patient, or that we are able to offer some form of help that is acceptable and useful. Dr Peter Sainsbury's study (1975) takes the view that the majority are amenable to treatment and most are incapable of making any useful decision. He states:

> The view that healthy people kill themselves, and justifiably do so if circumstances are sufficiently adverse, or that the individual should be free to decide his own fate, is not tenable to us.
> The protection of the suicide is as much a medical and community responsibility as any other cause of death against which prophylactic and therapeutic measures are available.

On the one hand, we have a sociological approach and on the other, a medical one. There must also be a political one, and we have some useful information and statistics for the politicians. Since my study in 1979, the numbers of self-poisoning patients had almost doubled by 1983. A significant change was that in 1978 almost two-thirds of the patients were women; in 1983, half were men. Alongside the increase in self-poisoning in relatively young men was a dramatic increase in unemployment and marital breakdown. Frood's study (1982) showed that self-poisoning accounted for 17.5% of all medical admissions covered; 75% of the agents used were only available on prescription, and we know that 50% or more had seen their General Practitioner about their unhappiness.

Although these and other studies have highlighted those at risk, the problem continues. One would have thought that General Practitioners and others in the primary care team would have more awareness of who was at risk. However, if the problem is not a medical one, but sociological or political, why should GPs be cornered into making patients of these people? There must also be a large number of patients who have unrealistic expectations about what the doctor or his medication can achieve.

This, then, is the problem. Perhaps some of the nurses' ambivalent feelings about these patients are a result of their being left to sort out problems which are only in part medical, and are in part sociological and political as well. Sometimes, a day spent hearing the problems of these patients leaves you feeling you need to be psychotherapist, psychiatrist, social worker, politician, priest and philosopher. This multifactorial aspect presented by the self-poisoning patient must account for the opinion sometimes expressed by nurses that it is someone else's problem.

CHANNELS OF COMMUNICATION

So many aspects of this problem are concerned with communication: how the patient has related to other significant people in his life, and how we relate to the patient in the management of the crisis. Bowlby (1981) gives two reasons for a suicidal gesture:

1. A wish to elicit a caregiving response from an attachment figure who is felt to be neglectful (the well-known cry for help).
2. A wish to punish an attachment figure and so coerce him or her into being more attentive.

In any one act, one or more of these motives may play a part of may be combined with others. The usual channels of communication may not have been used, or the feelings may have been difficult to communicate.

In most cases, suicidal reactions involve feelings of hopelessness and helplessness related to the loss of or separation from a significant and valued person. The loss can be actual or impending. The behaviour can be seen as an expression of intense feelings when other forms of communication or expression have failed. The individual feels unable to cope with the despair and intensity of feelings, and believes that others are not aware of his pain, nor are they responding to his needs. The patient may verbalize this and say 'I no longer want to live.' or 'Let me kill myself.'

Most patients are in the Accident and Emergency Department within 1 hour of taking the drugs. The amount of the drug taken, or its potential to kill, may bear no relation to the suicidal risk or intention to harm. The intensity of feelings expressed can be the same in the patient who has swallowed a few harmless antibiotics as in the patient who has taken a potentially lethal amount of paracetamol. During the first hour, most will express despair and hopelessness, but as time moves on the intensity may abate.

Many of you will be aware how, overnight, you have seen a dramatic change in the patient's mood and thoughts. This causes some difficulty for the nurse and leads her to question the patient's degree of motivation in attempting to kill himself. She may feel she has been involved in some sort of game that the patient has engineered.

The attempted suicide, and the obvious despair, indicate the low ebb the patient has reached when he is admitted. The following day he is aware that he was at his lowest and that nothing can be worse than that. He then begins to move away from the distress. He leaves the disorganisation that was discussed in Chapter 1 and sees alternatives, and directions in which to move. The ability to move and choose is powerful compared with being stuck with overwhelming feelings, so the next day is part of having moved forward and this explains some of the change that the nurse has difficulty with. In the patient's case the change will have been experienced, accepted, received and understood.

AMBIVALENCE

This facilitates a movement away from the crisis. Ambivalence is often present and expressed strongly, and is difficult to respond to. It is difficult for the patient, the family, and the nurse. How do you respond to 'I hate you.', 'Go away.', 'Please help me.', 'Tell me you care about me.', 'You don't care about anyone.' All these contradictions may be manifest in the behaviour you see or have heard about. It extends to the suicidal act: 'I want to die', followed by swallowing a hundred tablets to 'Please help me to live.' Some of the disorder witnessed and felt by you will distress you and will extend into your role and the way you function.

You should not feel you have failed if you feel threatened by this ambivalence and have difficulty with it. It is a reflection of what is happening to the patient and it may indicate you are in tune with his feelings.

HOSTILITY

The anger and hostility displayed by a large number of these patients alienates them from the staff. I believe there are good reasons for these emotions being a component of self-poisoning in most cases, but anger is felt to be inappropriate and not part of the total picture.

Before working in the Accident and Emergency Department I was a Charge Nurse on an acute psychiatric ward for 3 years. It was therefore of interest to me to see the difference in the patient on his arrival in the Accident and Emergency Department compared to 24–48 hours later when he was admitted to the psychiatric ward, often uncommunicative and miserable. His withdrawal into this passive state contrasted sharply with the anger displayed in the Accident and Emergency Department. In the ward, it would take someone's time and skills to locate the focus of the crisis and the emotions being felt. In the Accident and Emergency Department and on the acute medical ward the anger and focus are usually painfully obvious. The problem is that in those settings this is thought to be an inappropriate way to behave, but in looking at this hostility and anger, perhaps we should consider how the patient came to be here.

THE JOURNEY TO AND THROUGH THE HOSPITAL

This journey is fraught with many difficulties and consideration of these may increase our empathy for the patient.

On feeling desperate, the patient seeks help from a local GP, who may have little training, experience or skills to deal with the problem. It may be a problem that needs skilled counselling or crisis intervention, but after a short consultation it may be felt that some medication is necessary. Anxiolytic drugs are likely to be prescribed. The studies previously mentioned indicate how diazepam and lorazepam and other benzodiazepines are often the drug of choice. Studies have shown that these drugs can release hitherto controlled emotions and allow hostility to emerge. This produces problems with relationships and makes individuals aware of previously internalised feelings, which may be of despair and misery. Hall & Joffe (1972) reported how patients developed insomnia and depression which led to suicidal ideas, after being prescribed these drugs. The drugs do not mix well with alcohol and cause patients to lose control of their emotions.

Consider, then, that some of the feelings expressed may be due to the medication prescribed by the patient's GP.

In my study, 99% of the patients came to hospital by ambulance as emergencies. It is difficult for ambulance personnel to be objective about patients with self-inflicted problems when they could be collecting an injured child from a road accident. The patient may well have been told this quite forcefully.

On arrival in the Accident and Emergency Department many questions will be asked about the poisoning. Remember that at this stage, the patient is still in an emotional crisis, and patients are often irritated by the details required concerning the poisoning. The Department may be full of other emergencies. Remember that child from the traffic accident — he will need immediate attention. It will be difficult not to convey the opinion that the child deserves help more than the patient who has taken an overdose.

The patient will probably need a stomach washout. Many will resist this and become very angry. It is a distateful procedure which is also messy. The patient may vomit round the tube and onto the nurses' legs and feet. Vomit may well end up in the patient's hair and on his face, and specimens of vomit will be saved for analysis. The room may stink of alcohol and vomit. When the procedure is over the patient will feel even worse about himself and his situation, and will often be apologetic that you, the nurse, have had to carry out the procedure.

What makes the procedure even worse is that its value is questionable. Proudfoot (1984) discusses how its use has limitations and common usage should not blind physicians to these limitations. Most paediatricians have abandoned its use in favour of emetics — a change which came about because gastric lavage causes phychological distress and because emetics are equally effective. In adults, it is often felt to be useful because it has a deterrent effect, but we should not be in this profession in order to be part of a system that condones punishment in the form of lavage or any other treatment. Gastric lavage is performed in order to retrieve a drug; some doctors fear legal repercussions if the procedure is not carried out and are concerned that they will be sued. It will be difficult to abandon the procedure.

From the Accident and Emergency Department the patient will be admitted to a medical ward or, in some hospitals, the Accident and Emergency short stay ward. On arrival in the medical ward the patient will be examined physically and questioned further about the poison and its effect. Remember he is still in crisis, and that crisis is not part of the concern of the medical ward staff but belongs to the social workers or the psychiatrist. So throughout the start of the patient's stay in hospital we ask him to shelve his emotional problems until the psychiatric team sees him the next day. This fragmentation of care interferes seriously with good communication with the patient and also asks the impossible of him.

In some centres the overall implications of the poisoning are treated from the beginning. The Accident and Emergency Department short stay ward is probably the best place to treat the patient. It means the staff have to facilitate all the necessary resources quickly as the beds are short stay. The staff on this unit are usually more comfortable with crisis, ambivalence and disruption. They are more likely to have a good working relationship with the psychiatrist. The staff can also observe the patient's responses from his admission in the Accident and Emergency Department until his discharge, because he remains in that department's care.

You will see that for the patient, his stay in and journey through various aspects of health care are fraught with many problems. Many aspects of his care will be harmful to him and will work against positive intervention.

EVALUATING THE SUICIDAL RISK

If we look at the statistics for those who successfully commit suicide, the rate increases with age in both sexes, but in both groups male rates exceed the female rates. The highest and lowest economic groups have a raised incidence according to the figures of the Registrar General. The suicide rate is associated with divorce, bereavement and urban residence. Most completed suicides have a history of mental illness; a higher incidence occurs in depressives and chronic alcoholics.

People who attempt suicides display different characteristics. Often the person involved is much younger and makes the attempt on impulse as a means of communicating anger or showing some other person how he is feeling. It may also be a way of providing a respite from an unpleasant, emotionally disturbing situation or change. The act is carried out so that discovery is inevitable and the chief method of using mild sedative drugs has a reduced likelihood of resulting in death. In contrast, the methods used in the successful suicide are more deliberate and carefully planned. Care is taken to avoid detection and the methods may be more violent and instantaneous such as shooting or hanging.

To evaluate the risk it would be important to take a detailed history of the events surrounding the act. Age, sex and any previous history of mental illness are also important considerations to take into account.

Some nurses will find the use of tables and scales for scoring the risk to be a more objective approach. These will help with setting boundaries for assessment, and relieve some of the anxiety about making the right decision. One example is the Beck Suicidal Intent Scale (Beck 1974) shown in Table 5.1, where the risk is evaluated on how the patient scores. It also means we have to rely on memory when considering pertinent aspects of the act. This scale also helps in evaluating attitudes and feelings.

The prediction of suicide is not easy. The most experienced nurses can be misled in their assessment. Looking after suicidal patients over a number of years means that you may well have experienced the death of one or more of them, and this can be felt to be a heavy responsibility, a factor which must contribute to this type of patient being unpopular.

Any plan for intervention must include the prevention of suicide and the patient's suicide potential. We have already discussed incidence and aetiology. As well as being familiar with current trends relating to suicide it is useful to have a methodical approach towards evaluating suicide. Keeping these points in mind, consider Table 5.2.

Table 5.1 Beck Suicidal Attempt Scale

Part 1 Objective circumstances relating to suicide attempt

Isolation

0 Someone present
1 Someone nearby in visual or vocal contact
2 No-one nearby or in visual or vocal contact

Timing

0 Intervention probable
1 Intervention unlikely
2 Intervention highly unlikely

Precautions against discovery/intervention

0 No precautions
1 Passive precautions, e.g. avoiding others but doing nothing to prevent their intervention: alone in a room with unlocked door
2 Active precautions, e.g. locked door

Acting to get help during/after attempt

0 Notified potential helper regarding attempt
1 Contacted but did not specifically notify potential helper regarding attempt
2 Did not contact or notify potential helper

Final acts in anticipation of death, e.g. will, gifts, insurance

0 None
1 Thought about or made some arrangements
2 Made definite plans or contemplated arrangements

Active preparation for attempt

0 None
1 Minimal
2 Extensive

Suicide note

0 Absence of note
1 Note written but torn up, or thought about
2 Absence of note

Overt communication of intent before the attempt

0 None
1 Equivocal communication
2 Unequivocal communication

Part 2 Self report

Alleged purpose of attempt

0 To manipulate environment, get attention, revenge
1 Components of 0 and 2
2 To escape, solve problems

Table 5.1 Beck Suicidal Attempt Scale (*contd*)

Expectations of fatality

0 Thought that death was unlikely
1 Thought that death was possible but not probable
2 Thought that death was probable or certain

Conception of method's lethality

0 Did less to self than thought would be lethal
1 Was unsure if action would be lethal
2 Equalled or exceeded what he thought would be lethal

Seriousness of attempt

0 Did not seriously attempt to end life
1 Uncertain about seriousness to end life
2 Seriously attempted to end life

Attitude towards living/dying

0 Did not want to die
1 Components of 0 and 2
2 Wanted to die

Conception of medical rescuability

0 Thought that death would be unlikely with medical attention
1 Was uncertain whether death could be averted by medical attention
2 Was certain of death even with medical attention

Degree of premeditation

0 None, impulsive
1 Contemplated for 3 hours or less before attempt
2 Contemplated for more than 3 hours before attempt

Table 5.2 Incidence and aetiology in assessing risk

Think about	Short evaluation
Age and sex	
Were plans made or was it on impulse?	
Was there a significant loss — death, divorce, unemployment etc?	
Clinical signs of mental illness	
Past methods of coping	
Resources — of patient and others of significance	
How is all this communicated?	

FACILITATING GOOD COMMUNICATION

We have already discussed how poor communication plays a major part in attempted suicide. The following components of the interaction appear to be significant in establishing a good rapport with the patient.

1. Take the threats seriously. Although the threat may appear inappropriate to you and out of proportion to the situation, it can be a sign of desperation. If you play it down, the patient may have to take further desperate measures to make you aware of the gravity of the situation.
2. Try not to be judgemental. This produces hostility which results in impulsive responses, and is the one aspect about which patients constantly complain when there has been a disagreement between a doctor or nurse and the patient. Some of the most judgemental responses are unspoken.
3. Stay and work on the feelings you are presented with at that time. Remarks to the effect that it is not really that bad, or that in the morning things will be all right, are steering away from the patient's present position. This may also be an unrealistic response as the factors leading to the attempted suicide may be exactly the same when the patient leaves hospital. The way he copes and the resources available to him will be the factors that may change.
4. Work with the positive aspects, and reinforce them in a realistic way. So much of what has happened is destructive and negative, and the recognition and affirmation of the person underneath all this destructive behaviour are steps in a positive direction. When the patient begins to talk about the suicide, tell him how useful this is and how difficult it can be.
5. Accept that anger, on the part of the patient or his family, is a major component of attempted suicide. The suggestion that anger is inappropriate will produce difficulties. Anger is useful in the discharge of strong emotions, but the hostility should not turn into violence. You have a need to protect yourself and a duty to protect other members of staff, and you may also have other vulnerable patients and relatives in the vicinity and be aware of the need to protect them. A private, comfortable room in which to talk is essential.

6. Keep in mind the fact that the poisoning may cause physical problems. Remain alert for signs that the patient's physical condition is deteriorating. Encourage oral fluids while you are talking.

ASPECTS THAT RESULT IN ANXIETY FOR STAFF

You may suddenly become aware that you are alone with the crisis, isolated from colleagues, and this may add to your anxiety and prevent concentration if the patient becomes hostile. It is better that the room has a window in it, so that you can look out. It is reassuring to know that colleagues are near. The hostility is frightening and can be incapacitating — patients can be homicidal as well as suicidal. Don't be brave if someone is armed with a razor, a bottle or a knife. An attempt to resolve the situation quickly may have disastrous consequences, so concentrate on establishing rapport.

A constant fear for staff is that they will be blamed if a patient leaves the hospital when he is still suicidal. Some patients will insist on leaving and you have no grounds to detain them. If you have taken reasonable measures with the resources available to you, there will be no criticism and your efforts will be regarded in a sympathetic light. If the patient has insight into the implications, he must take the ultimate responsibility.

There are some ethical dilemmas connected with the treatment of the psycopathic patient when he presents with self-inflicted injury or self-poisoning. The Mental Health (Amendment) Act 1983 for England and Wales states:

> In the case of psycopathic disorder or mental impairment such treatment is likely to alleviate or prevent a deterioration of his condition.

If the condition is not amenable to treatment, therefore, there is no reason to detain the patient. You may make the assumption from this that detention does not result from the immediate problem we are presented with, but from our prediction of the outcome of any treatment. This change in the law emphasises that responsibility for themselves is being handed back to the patients.

It will be obvious by now that the considerations in the

management of the patient are many, and that anxiety is caused for the staff because the responsibility is so great. Fortunately for the nurse, the responsibility is not hers alone although in the team approach her opinion may be sought. A team response shares decision-making and responsibility and is therefore supportive for the staff.

THE REPEATED ATTENDER

Only a minority of our patients are psychopathic or are diagnosed as having personality disorders. These few often present to the hospital repeatedly, and cause management problems. The lifestyle of these people means that they experience recurrent crises; they refuse to focus on or work with the problem, and so the unresolved conflict means a recurrence of the same problems. They often harm themselves, frequently get into fights, and clash with the law. One way to avoid the law temporarily, or to avoid the problem for the time being, is to become a health problem or someone else's responsibility. The Health Service has 24-hour access for emergencies, and for this reason and in order to avoid the real issue, these people will often become patients.

You will know by contact or reputation the patient who persistently lacerates his wrists or arms. This behaviour produces immediate attention and dramatic disruption. To witness someone lacerating his arms and to see him with gaping wounds and dripping blood evokes strong feelings in the observer — these reactions can be pity, dismay, anger, helplessness or flight. When hospital personnel have to spend hours suturing this patient and he is ungrateful and abusive, feelings will arise in the staff which are difficult to control. You may find it hard to understand what he wants. Through all the hostility and disruption, it may be necessary to try to sort out some clear messages:

'What do you want?'
'Tell me what you are asking me or us to do.'

If his needs are unrealistic or cannot be met, make this clear in your reply, or you will be confronted later with any deviation from complete honesty. False promises must be avoided. Because of the lifestyle of these patients, and their responses to stress, they will often become hospital patients and for this reason some sort of dialogue is necessary. No matter how you feel about this disjointed and disruptive behaviour, or whether the Health Service should need to sort them out, your paths will cross many times. If this is inevitable, some rapport and dialogue will improve the management and intervention for you.

The problem is that patients comprising this small group who repeatedly attempt suicide by self-poisoning or wrist-slashing, are at risk of subsequent suicide. Wrist-slashing often appears to alleviate intolerable tension and is often carried out in a state of detachment. For these patients, intensive short-term intervention appears ineffective. Long-term support may be the only way of reducing the frequency of attempts. Another approach that can be useful is an analysis of the patient's behaviour, in order to evaluate the benefits he receives from these repeated attempts.

THE DRUG- OR ALCOHOL-DEPENDENT PATIENT

Some patients are referred to hospital because they have been found drowsy or unconscious. There may have been alcohol or drug containers at the scene.

Assumptions could be made that the patient has attempted suicide, and it may be more acceptable for him if he is thought of in this way rather than being labelled a drug or alcohol abuser. Signs of the downward spiral of the drug/alcohol abuser should be looked for — a dirty and neglected condition with signs of malnutrition and muscle wasting. Check the ante-cupital fossa for signs of needle marks, or the front of the upper legs or ankle veins. There may be signs of jaundice. Check clothing for loose tablets or capsules.

Many of these people, who have no fixed abode or who sleep on the streets, take a mixture of drugs and alcohol, which can be a cheaper way of gaining oblivion. Repeated episodes of drowsiness and unconsciousness may need some confrontation about abuse rather than about attempted suicide. Automatically to assume attempted suicide and explore this further means an ineffective intervention, and, for the worker, a strong sense that there is no real crisis on which to work. It is often a relief for the patient when someone confronts him with the real focus of his problem. It also means a referral to the correct agency and a better chance of creating an effective strategy to put things right.

DEALING WITH THE FAMILY

The family or loved ones of a self-poisoning patient may have waited on their own for a long time in the hospital. Because they feel embarrassed or responsible they often choose not to get the support of other family members or friends. Some wait silently, and are preoccupied with why, and whether they could have prevented this. Others are restless and agitated and demand constant updating as to the condition of the patient.

You will be familiar with the defensive response, and the assurances that the patient is loved and wanted. Some will blame the General Practitioner for prescribing the drugs or for failing to see the potential suicidal risk. The most difficult response is the denial, or 'Let's just try to forget the whole thing.' The attempt leaves the family/loved one embarrassed, scared and perplexed. So many questions are unanswered and these bewildered relatives do not know where to begin.

Encourage them to discuss and confront the issues and remind them that when the patient leaves hospital the problem will not have magically disappeared. It is important that the patient has the concern and support of the family or loved one when he leaves hospital. Remember from Chapter 1 the emphasis to be placed on situational support — this can be the vital component that tips the balance towards effective intervention.

A difficult situation can arise when the patient shares with the nurse the reasons for his attempted suicide. The family will often seek enlightenment from the nurse as to the precipitating factors. When you see the family feeling so guilty and perplexed, you may be tempted to share this information with them in order to put them out of their misery. The information exchanged between you and the patient is confidential, and it is important that you retain his trust and confidence. It is better that the patient himself reveals to the family the motives behind the act. Some patients will ask to do this in the presence of the nurse or psychiatrist as they are afraid they will be unable to cope with the response. The hospital is often regarded as a safe place in which to reveal some terrible problem or difficulty.

It is not unusual for the family or friends to be extremely hostile and difficult because they are aware that the nurse has some knowledge about the patient that they do not have. Although this results in demanding and disruptive responses at times, it is an ethic which we need to guard carefully. It may even alienate you from the police who demand too much information or ask you to break confidences. Your response to the family of the attempted suicide has powerful repercussions because they themselves may become patients or need to share a confidence with Health Service staff.

It is difficult not to react personally to the patient's provocative behaviour. Keep yourself aware of his ambivalence and of the way his erratic response is a reflection of his difficulties. Being stuck with a problem, and not knowing in which direction to move, may produce impulsive and erratic behaviour. Remember to respond to the feelings, and ask yourself how his behaviour reflects them. If you remain aware of the risk factors, your level of anxiety and your feelings of helplessness and hopelessness will be reduced.

The skills which are necessary to locate the person beneath some of the difficult behaviour remain a challenge, and any increase in our effectiveness has many implications which are not immediately obvious. The amount of misery, and the financial drain on Health Service resources, caused by the self-poisoning patient is enormous. The size of the problem should not eliminate the possibility of useful interaction by two or three people or of our own individual effectiveness or humanity.

Case study

When the ambulance got to Elizabeth's home, her 10-year-old son was crying in the garden. He told the crew that his Mummy was upstairs poorly and she had asked him to ring for an ambulance. She was lying fully clothed on the bed. Beside her was an empty sherry bottle and an empty tablet container. The container had Elizabeth's name on and was marked 'Diazepam 5 mg'. She was obviously drunk and laughed when they entered the room. The son appeared behind the crew and announced that his Mummy had taken a lot of tablets. He knew that the bottle had been full that morning.

No neighbours could be seen, and the ambulance men discovered that any relatives lived miles away. Elizabeth then became abusive and demanded that her son accompany her to the hospital. When they lifted her onto the trolley she became more hostile, called them pigs, and said that all men were the same. On the way to the hospital in the ambulance, conversation was limited. John, who was obviously embarrassed at his mother's behaviour, talked to compensate for this and to distract attention from his mother.

Her arrival at the Accident and Emergency Department was ill-timed, as the staff were busy with three patients from a hit and run accident. A child was screaming in the background. The nurse who received Elizabeth seemed to be more concerned about John, and enquired where his father was. Elizabeth made some disparaging remarks about him being in the golf club. She was becoming more and more agitated and was unable to sit or lie still.

When the ambulance crew gave details of her condition, they emphasised how disgusting her behaviour had been and how they were concerned about its effect on the child. Elizabeth became angry, aware that they were talking about her. The staff nurse told her to behave herself and reminded her that she was embarrassing her son; she went on to say that many of the patients were really ill through no fault of their own. Before Elizabeth could speak the nurse left the room and took John with her. In the background, telephones were ringing, children crying, and some staff were laughing, Elizabeth heard two female voices bemoaning the fact that they would be late off duty and might miss a party.

Elizabeth felt bad about John and wanted to say how sorry she was, but he had been taken away. Tears of sorrow, anger and frustration welled up inside her. Her husband, Mike, would be at the golf club enjoying himself. Everything good came his way; he mixed in the right circles and was popular, while she stayed at home, just a glorified house-keeper, feeling drab and unloved. She wished she could tell him how she felt a failure because she could not get pregnant again for him. He avoided the subject. He avoided it in the same way that she avoided discussing the fact that she drank a bottle of sherry every day.

It seemed to Elizabeth that the real issues were avoided by all and sundry. In her 5 minutes with her General Practitioner, she had not had time to tell him she thought Mike had a girl friend, and that she was frightened both for the future and about the intensity of her feelings.

Elizabeth then began to sob and cry like she had never done before, loudly and uncontrollably. She could usually stop it but not this time. Another nurse walked in and asked her to keep calm, 'because the others could hear her.'

'To hell with the others' was Elizabeth's response, and the nurse left. Her anger had given Elizabeth some new-found energy — noisily she raised herself from the trolley and found her clothes. She was overwhelmed by the feeling that no-one would listen to the full story. She never quite finished it. Perhaps she did not deserve to be heard or helped. She was a bad mother and a bad person, and less deserving than these other people. Although surrounded by people, she was the loneliest person in the world, and the least deserving.

QUESTIONS FOR DISCUSSION

1. How do we avoid being judgemental?
2. How do we now establish some rapport with Elizabeth?
3. Answer the statement that this patient's behaviour was totally inappropriate.
4. Discuss 'responsibility' in the event of a patient's suicide, and how this influences our performance.

REFERENCES

Beck A T 1974 The prediction of suicide. In: Beck A T, Resnik H P, Lettierie D (eds) Charles Press, New York
Bowlby J 1981 Attachment and loss, vol 3. Penguin, Hamondsworth

Durkheim E 1975 Suicide — A study in sociology. Routledge & Keagan Paul, London

Frood R A W 1982 Poisoning in East Cheshire. Update 24:6

Hall R C W, Joffe J R 1972 Aberrant response to diazepam. American Journal of Psychiatry 129:6

Proudfoot A T 1984 Abandon gastric lavage in the Accident and Emergency Department. Archives of Emergency Medicine 2: 65–67

Roberts D 1984 Non-verbal communication. Popular and unpopular patients. In: Faulkner A (ed) Communication. Recent Advances in Nursing Churchill Livingstone, Edinburgh

Sainsbury P 1975 A Handbook of the study of suicide. Oxford University Press, Oxford

Wright B 1979 Self poisoning — its trends and management. Nursing Times 75:46

6

Victims of violence

There are many things we do not know about our own aggression and the violence in society, but what we do know as workers in a health care system is that violence and aggression produce a great deal of misery in human terms and a great deal of suffering in physical terms. The end result of this violence, i.e. the injury, is becoming an increasing part of our patient care. Many of you will have witnessed both the physical and emotional damage to the patient, his family and friends. The effects do not remain there but spread like ripples in a pool to produce more hostility and violence, the effects of which are profoundly disturbing and damaging.

Before we consider how to minimise this damage in our total care of the patient, it is worthwhile considering the theories about, and settings in which, violence occurs.

VIOLENCE IN SOCIETY

In his book *The Strange History of Bonnie and Clyde*, John Treherne (1984) attempts to explain how these two vicious, psychopathic killers came to be admired and romanticized throughout America. News of their exploits filled many people with excitement and admiration. If you saw the film, you may have pondered how the love, romance and adventure could be reconciled with the violence and blood spilling. It is suggested in the book that the attraction came at a time of depression and gloom in the economy when people needed a distraction.

The concept of what constitutes violence is full of hypocrisy and confusion. A man may condemn two men fighting in the street and label them animals, but later he may pay a substantial amount of money for a ticket to a boxing match, and shout with excitement and discuss the boxers' skills, even when one of them sustains brain damage and is at risk of dying.

Gilbert Geis (1982) asks 'Does the willed or known or anticipated consequence of an act of commission or omission determine its violent or non violent nature?' He argues that the passivity of onlookers at a violent act may be just as violent as the perpetrator's. He also discusses how the outcome of the act may then determine our judgement of whether it is violence or not. The punch that is thrown and misses may be acceptable, whereas the one that knocks someone down may be violent.

In discussing the origins of violence, Eysenck (1979) outlines the various hypotheses put forward to explain its existence in present day society. His conclusions are that social and biological factors are responsible, but he emphasises the need to develop a conscience. This is done in children through conditioning, and is necessary in order to control violent responses.

The Russells (1979) cite studies of monkeys who are relaxed under spacious conditions with reduced episodes of quarrelling, whereas crowded monkeys have brutal bosses, and wound and often kill each other. The effect of crowding in other mammals produces similar results. The Russells go on to describe how human beings need ample space and how overcrowding produces violence. They discuss the way in which resources become stretched in crowded urban areas, producing stress and resulting in violence.

Violence manifests itself daily in hospital Accident and Emergency Departments as a result of road traffic accidents, acts of violence associated with crime and mental disturbance, and battering of wives and children. We can perhaps relate some of these to lack of space and overcrowding, but we are also aware, from our nteraction with others, that some people do not appear to have developed a conscience.

You may wonder, when considering the many factors that produce violence and our many different responses to it, whether this overview of it is pointless. It could be argued that violence will always be a part of our nature and society. I think it is important to look at the reasons why, and to try to understand the factors that trigger this sort of response. We may have information that lies behind the statistics of our injured or maimed which could aid reforms, and we are in a unique position to monitor trends and attitudes. It could be argued that violence is inherent within us and for this reason we avoid confronting the issue.

Dixon & Lucas (1982) discuss how the link between crime and violence is overemphasised. Most of the violent offences recorded in Britain stem from disputes between relatives or people who know each other well. These offences occur in predictable locations such as private homes, pubs and dance halls, and they rarely involve dangerous weapons. You may have great difficulty intervening in these situations. The truth is that we ourselves can identify closely with many of them and it may be that we avoid the issue for this reason. There is also the idea that this area of a relationship is private and we are reluctant to be seen interfering. We would not like to be identified as busybodies.

I believe that many of our patients who are victims of violence are going to grasp this opportunity to seek help. You will have heard the response to the effect that 'Now is time to deal with the issue.' Before we look at specific problems associated with violence, we should explore what it means to be the victim.

THE VICTIM

The Shorter Oxford English Dictionary (Onions 1983) contains the following definitions of victim:

1. A living creature killed and offered as a sacrifice to some deity or supernatural power (1497).

2. A person who is put to death or subjected to torture by another; one who suffers severely in body or property through cruel or oppressive treatment (1660).

3. One who is reduced or destined to suffer under some oppressive or destructive agency (1718).

4. One who perishes or suffers in health for some enterprise or pursuit voluntarily undertaken (1726).

5. In weaker sense: One who suffers some injury or hardship or loss, is badly treated or taken advantage of or the like (1781).

I find these definitions a useful way of exploring what we mean by 'the victim' because they give us some insight into the responses with which we are faced. Most people view the world as a safe and pleasant place in which people have control over their lives. When a violent episode occurs at the hands of another person, the victim's view of himself and those around him is changed.

Immediately after the incident the victim becomes withdrawn or inaccessible, and may appear apathetic about the ultimate outcome of the whole affair. The feeling that he has control over his life will be gone; most feel that the event could recur and that they will be helpless to prevent this. You may witness short episodes of anger, with striking out. Robbery or burglary victims, if not injured, can feel contaminated and therefore damaged because their property has been invaded and handled by strangers.

The dictionary descriptions of the feelings associated with victims are particularly useful in increasing our empathy. Think of the words 'cruel' and 'sacrificial' in association with a higher power. This conveys strongly the suggestion that the victim is no longer in control; the word oppressive conveys very aptly the crushing and diminishing feelings. The aspect of being reduced or destined to suffer is interesting — some people slip very quickly into the passive role of victim and may need to be confronted with why they want to stay there.

The definition that describes someone as 'suffering after pursuing an enterprise voluntarily' places another interpretation on the role of victim. We often hear how a person was undertaking something with the best intention and then this terrible thing has to happen. You are being reminded that the victim did not invite or deserve this attack, and if the response is repeated or emphasised, ask yourself whether you may have suggested that the victim invited this violence.

The last part of the definition mentions being taken advantage of. This is the aspect that suggests to the victim that he has been stupid or gullible or is in some way to blame. The underlying message is that only someone stupid could get themselves into this situation.

The whole message about the victim is judgemental — he is not only full of self-judgement but will have the impression that you are judging him. If we have been foolish or acted irresponsibly in some way, we may feel it is better to withdraw and keep quiet, that we have already made a mess of things without making it worse. This may be why the victim appears unhelpful or just unresponsive; instead of demanding revenge he may demand nothing and appear passive and unresponsive.

When passivity occurs in women who have been assaulted by husbands, it produces an angry response in nurses, who cannot understand that the woman may feel judged and to blame. The opposite response would be vociferously defending her part in the dispute and emphasising that she was not to blame. Certain points may be laboured and reiterated to confirm that it was the fault of the other person and that she was the innocent victim.

Being the victim produces strong feelings and disadvantages, and the unhappiness it produces encompasses all aspects of that person's life at that time. Irrational though it may be, the feelings permeate into all aspects of the victim's life. Intervention is concerned with handling the focus, anger and all-embracing implications. We will look at some 'victims of violence' you will encounter in our health care system, and explore some of their particular needs.

CHILD ASSAULT

One of the most difficult tasks for health care staff is dealing with the problem of the battered child. These victims of violence produce strong and disturbing feelings in those who hear about them. Because of a child's vulnerability and defencelessness we have a strong need to speak on his behalf. In defending the child, i.e. being the victim's advocate, it is difficult not to get involved in areas of revenge and punishment. We are then confronted with some very powerful feelings, and may be disturbed by the hostility of our own response. All this can cause a lot of anxiety for us when we consider our objectivity in handling these cases.

Staff who have mismanaged or failed to recognise an act of abuse may be castigated publicly and in the press. This other dimension can make the whole management fraught with anxiety, and this is one reason why the team approach shares the burden by allowing a place to air strong views and feelings.

Parents who abuse children are often immature people who are unable to cope with their own stress and hostility. The child may be felt to be the reason for their being in some disturbing or difficult situation, or the parents may feel the child is preventing the resolution of some problem or is preventing movement away from it. Low income, poor housing, or unemployment may be underlying the rage that is then heaped upon the child. Although parents recognise that the hostility is triggered by all or many of these factors, the strength of feelings still leads to the aggressive behaviour.

Most people will give you advice on how child-batterers should be punished. It is easy to be an expert when the problem has been recognised and the aggression admitted. Recognition of the abuse is a very difficult problem — imagine the consequences if you get it wrong. Because of the legal implications, the social implications (the child may be placed in care) and the need to invade private family matters, the whole scene may be avoided. Involvement in this area reminds us that much of our work involves 'risk taking'.

Below, I will look briefly at some of the psychological approaches that can be made by the staff in this kind of individual and family crisis. Work by Penny Tokarski (1982) and many others will provide information about the physical signs to look out for and the medical examination to be carried out.

Taking the history

Again, I think, you should first identify what your underlying feelings are when taking the history from parents. You will not want to frighten them away by questioning them in an intimidating or threatening manner. You will not want them to get up suddenly, take the child and leave your ward, clinic or department. There is more pressure than usual to set the right tone here, and to establish some rapport with the parents. You need their co-operation, not alienation; if you get it wrong, you may not get the evidence you need. It is therefore important to get the approach right.

In the Emergency Department, someone may have an opportunity to talk to the parents while the child is taken to X-ray accompanied by a nurse. At this separation, remind the child that he will see Mummy or Daddy again shortly. This not only reassures the child but reminds the parents that you have not begun the process of taking the child from them. It is important to find a quiet room where conversations are not overheard. This in itself will facilitate disclosure and the privacy will allow painful or strong feelings to emerge. It will be necessary for you to talk calmly and in a non-judgemental way, which may not be easy. You should acknowledge that you may have difficulty with this and if necessary, ask someone to take over from you. If the parents become defensive, it may prevent them from accepting help not only from you, but from other health care professionals. Imposing your own values or firing questions at them can be intimidating and may produce a need on their behalf to have more space.

With gentle questioning and time allowed for the salient points to emerge, you may get the information you need. It may then be possible to get on to the subject of how stressful it can be to be a parent. It may even be possible to explore this further by inviting responses to such topics as how much patience we need when children push us to our limits. Discussion about how much time and commitment children demand may produce responses that have a strength of feeling enough to give us some indication of the family's stress.

None of this is easy and may produce a strong sense of urgency, but by rushing this area of the work, you may lose contact with the parents and the child. In taking the history, some insight into our own underlying feelings may help us with our objectivity.

Talking to the child

It is often easier to get children to talk when you are doing something for them, such as applying a dressing or immobilising a fracture. It is somehow less of a confrontation, and allows certain issues to be raised incidental to the main task. This is the only additional observation I would make to my original seven guidelines (Wright 1981) which are:

1. Try to talk to the child alone, to establish some rapport with him.
2. Be less direct — show an interest in his book, toy, where he lives. Be gentle without being overindulgent: children from disturbed families are sensitive to manoeuvres.
3. Encourage the child to introduce the topic of conversation. Do not, for example, say 'Did your Dad hit you?' Try 'What are you thinking about?'
4. What we would consider to be abnormally aggressive behaviour in these families may be normal to the child. Look for signs of guilt in his manner and demeanour. Sadly some of these children feel they deserve the punishment.
5. Tread carefully. Many children will have great difficulty in being disloyal to those closest to them.
6. Do not jump to conclusions. Many children are abused by cohabitees, stepfathers, baby sitters, close family friends and neighbours. The extended family, such as uncles or grandparents, are not immune. It may not be the person who is accompanying the child.
7. If they do not want to talk, do not push them too hard. You will lose them. It is worthwhile waiting.

It is always wise in any suspected case of battering to request details of all previous hospitalizations and previous visits to Emergency Departments. One study (Hight et al 1979) showed that of 40 children admitted to hospital with abuse-related medical problems, 37% had had previous visits with related problems. In the long-term, it is also important to include in your assessment previous contact with other agencies, especially the family GP.

Give plenty of consideration to explanations that the child is accident prone, clumsy, or that he 'bruises easily'. In any event, this will need medical investigation. Injuries described as self-inflicted may not be possible in a child of that age. Underweight children may be described as 'failure to thrive' and you may detect signs of psychological or emotional disturbance.

Child abuse and neglect can produce crisis in individuals or the family as a whole because, although resulting in an obvious chronic condition, detection and confrontation produce panic and fear.

It is important to bear in mind that the way the situation is handled may produce very powerful and disruptive responses among members of the health care team dealing with the problem.

VIOLENCE AGAINST WOMEN

Many health care workers, particularly Emergency Department staff, are aware of the high numbers of women who are assaulted. Most of these assaults occur within a domestic setting, being inflicted by the spouse — you will hear police and other staff refer to the patient as a 'domestic incident'. This label of 'domestic incident' often means that less importance will be given to the occurrence, despite the fact that the victim often receives serious physical injury. This, along with the implications of being violated which were discussed earlier, can have a seriously damaging effect on the individual who will then be at a disadvantage. Initially, there- fore, it is important to look at the way we and society look at women who have been violated:

1. There is an underlying idea that what happens within the family is sacred. We are reluctant to invade the privacy of the family. We may also fear a strong rebuff from the victim.

2. Cultural norms suggest that women are chattels and the property of men. Jean Orr (1984) goes further by asking why we choose to label these victims 'wives' rather than the mugged, murdered or assaulted. The crime is, in some way, different, even though the outcome is the same. It is within

the family that we learn sexual stereotyping of masculinity and femininity — men dominate and are in control and strong; women take a subservient role.

3. Many people blame the victim:

'She must have asked for it.'
'Some women like it.'
'She must have done something.'

This is further enlarged upon by many female health care workers asserting 'It would not happen to me.' This suggests that the victim is stupid or lacking in some skill to prevent it. This judgemental response is even stronger if it has happened before. Many people believe that we get what we deserve, and deny that the innocent can be violated, which makes them vulnerable.

4. The assailant may be very concerned and apologetic and it is easy to feel sorry for him. The victim may play down the incident for fear of further attack, and may accept society's stereotyping that she is in some way to blame and therefore makes light of the incident.

If we are to offer some help in these crises, we must again examine our own attitudes and responses. It is important that we make an effort to be objective and that we do not shift the patient's focus away from the problem. If you are persistently confronted with the sordid or distasteful, you may find that subconsciously, perhaps, you want to avoid the issue. I am not overstating the case when I say that to witness the damage and distress in these cases is sickening and obscene, and to try to avoid it is a natural reaction.

Responding to what confronts us

Having sorted out what may influence our objectiveness, what may confront us and how do we respond to it? Why should we respond at all? We know from crisis theory that intervention during the acute phase can prevent morbidity and promote resolution of the problem. When we confront the victim at this stage she is more amenable to suggestion and to working with the cause of the problem. Once she has left the Health Centre, Department or hospital without making a decision to seek change, she is unlikely to return.

In the study by Rounsaville (1978) only 35% of patients returned for help to the Emergency Department where help had been given initially. Effort was therefore made to use strategies that are successful or meaningful to the patient on the first visit. Some of these patients may have only had overnight admission, so we must invest some effort into this short transaction. For these reasons we will look at various ways in which we might respond to different aspects of the 'battered wife'.

1. Take a careful history of the event. Asking for factual information is easier to begin with, and it is less embarrassing than quickly exploring details of the relationship. If her memory is impaired and she is disorientated, this may not be the best time to intervene usefully in the implications of the crisis. Immediate treatment of the injuries is important, and after you have attended to the immediate needs of the patient you can move on to the next step.

2. Check hospital records for details or suggestions of previous episodes of domestic violence. You could use this as an opening for getting details of past occurrences. If you have no such details, you can say that in your experience it is not at all unusual for this sort of thing to have happened before. This makes the patient less of an oddity. Repeated previous visits for minor accidents should be viewed with suspicion if the patient now admits to having been assaulted.

3. Ask her about her previous medical history. Stark et al (1979) showed that these women had three times the number of abortions and twice the number of miscarriages. They are more likely to be pregnant when injured. The study also demonstrated how they present· with vague medical symptoms, suicide attempts and a persistent use. of tranquillizers.

4. Immediate focus on this event, on possible previous events and on general health problems may give some insight into the overall implications. If it does not, this may need to be clearly stated.

5. Some women may feel they deserve to be assaulted or maltreated or expect it. The long-term implications and dangers of this sort of environment need to be discussed.

6. The issues need to be shared sensitively and in a non-

judgemental way. The patient may be defensive about remarks made about her spouse. Concentrate on the needs of the person you are confronted with.

7. It is not easy financially or emotionally for a woman (especially when she has children) to leave her spouse. It is easy for the crisis worker to be angry about this and to be frustrated about the client's decision to stay. It is her decision alone. If she feels you do not understand the difficulties of this decision, your relationship with the patient will be damaged. It is possible to explain that any frustration you feel is due to your concern for her.

8. 'Ambivalence is difficult to work with' is a phrase I often repeat, and you will be faced with ambivalence frequently in domestic crises. Along with a great need for help and for an escape from the problem, you will see a dependence on the relationship. The passivity and resistance to change are appropriate, and to push too hard for sweeping changes may result in your losing rapport with the patient.

The perpetrator of the assault

Shortly after the violation has been committed or the spouse discovers his wife is in hospital, he may panic. He will want to get to her before she calls the police or implicates him to the hospital staff. He may want to reassure staff that it was all an accident. He may be repentent and beg forgiveness. Often, he is simply desperate to prevent further escalation of a terrible situation. When he confronts health staff he will, on the one hand, want to placate them about his role in the incident, and, on the other hand, need to see his wife urgently.

This agitation and need for a quick response may provoke further hostility and violence. We may be aware of his distress and keep him waiting, or we may be difficult and unco-operative because he deserves to suffer. There is no place for playing his sort of game, although I have sympathy for staff who do respond in this way. It is a response which is destructive for you, the patient and for all involved, and can lead to further violence.

The spouse will be keen to know what his wife has told you — but this can only be discussed by the patient, spouse and interventionist together. To divulge anything without the permission of the patient can put her in danger. When she is confronted by the spouse she may make a sudden decision not to proceed any further for help. If this is the outcome, she may not want him to know that the issues have already been discussed.

It should be recognised that many of these men have difficulty in discussing feelings. They may have poor verbal skills, or they may expound ideas, thoughts and philosophies about the role of spouses, wives and women that are totally alien to you. These problems are some of the most difficult and highly charged situations to work with, and present a strong challenge. If you can be effective in such a situation, it is very satisfying.

A warning

Sometimes a husband makes irrational, impulsive and violent responses to the suggestion that the spouse is taking measures to leave him. I have witnessed further violence being inflicted on wives and children, and children being snatched away. Any anxiety about the safety and welfare of children or wives who have left must be shared with the appropriate authority. If you fail to do this, ou are not only being remiss in your preventive medicine role, but also you may be held accountable if further harm befalls the family.

This can all be a heavy burden for you to bear personally — the authorities and media are usually happier if the finger of blame can be pointed at someone. The team approach makes for collective decision-making and for shared responsibility. It is easy for people to comment retrospectively on some of our responses, but health care staff will have to make decisions in a crisis when many other demands are being made upon them.

Health care staff working in acute care settings, especially emergency medicine, face the increasing challenge of offering comprehensive care for victims of domestic violence. It is clearly difficult to treat the injuries without paying heed to how they came about. Our understanding of the nature of the problem is important if we are to offer effective help.

RAPE AND SEXUAL ASSAULT

In the USA, where a woman is raped every 6–8 minutes, the probability of Emergency Department staff treating a rape victim is high. In the UK most victims are taken to the police station unless there is injury that requires hospital treatment. Nurses and other health care staff may, in other contexts, hear disclosures of rape or sexual abuse. The fact that the victim may be visited at home by the police, and may be taken away in a police car or have to visit a police station may put her at a further disadvantage, because this procedure seems to imply that we are more concerned with law and order than with the victim. The system I have witnessed in the USA, where victims are taken to an Emergency Department, implies concern about the health and care of the victim. When staff are correctly trained, this procedure does not prevent them from being aware of the legal aspects and the need to preserve clothing, etc., for clues and other implications.

Sensitive care of the victim is lost when the nurse finds herself wondering whether it was rape or seduction. This not only affects the way care is given, but also lies outside our role in the incident. You will all be able to cite cases where a woman makes a declaration of rape in order to explain or vindicate her sexual behaviour, or to implicate someone. Statistically, however, these cases are not common.

As we have already discussed, aggression is frighening, embarrassing and painful. Aggression combined with a sexual incident, which in itself can be embarrassing, compounds the horror of the experience. Sometimes, however, the embarrassment can be the worst feature. Although, in general, rape refers to forced vaginal intercourse experienced by women, forced anal penetration sustained by either male or female victims is also regarded as rape. Victims may feel too degraded or damaged to broach the subject and provide details. For this reason, the first indication that something like this has happened may be when a small clue is given, which the victim hopes you will pick up. For example:

'I thought he was going to kill me.'
'I should not have got myself there with him alone.'

Torn or damp clothing, scratches and bruises and

dishevelled hair and make-up may offer further clues. You do need to be alert to the fact that the victim may be too ashamed to present the rape or sexual abuse as the primary problem. In a study by the author (Wright 1983) carried out in the Leeds Accident and Emergency Department, it was demonstrated how patients often feel they have to present with a physical problem, when the real concern lies elsewhere. You can imagine how much more this applies if they have been raped or sexually abused. The patient may gather courage to disclose the facts and then, when confronted by the worker, change her mind. She may gauge your sensitivity by testing out whether you are alert to some clues.

Case study

Several years ago I saw a young girl aged 18 years, with several long red deep lines across her back, which were very painful. She described the excruciating pain when her clothes touched her back. The lesions were probably having crusted over. She explained that the marks had been caused by her slipping against some rose trees. On hearing this, the nurse became hostile because she felt she would be foolish to believe this.

I suggested that it would be very unusual for roses to produce this sort of injury, and asked her if it was possible that there was some other cause. 'I will have to think,' was the girl's reply. She was not thinking of another improbable answer but was wondering whether we were people with whom she could share the truth. I sensed she was attempting to evaluate our empathy, and after a period of silence I said 'It's amazing what some people will inflict upon others.'

'You've got it, but so what?' she replied reluctantly.

There was some relief at the disclosure, but some hostility that we were talking about her. She went on to say how her cohabitee received some sexual gratification out of inflicting pain upon her, and how he had lost control. This act culminated in her being raped. Her tears arose from her anger and her degradation at being a victim. She refused offers of help to call the police or any other worker. In an attempt to restore herself to her former dignity and status she became defensive and abusive:

'What do you all know about life?'
'What has it got to do with anyone else?'
'How do you know I didn't like it?'

Her defensiveness and ambivalence were difficult to cope with, both for her and for us. We explained to her that this was just how people reacted when something like this happened to them. One response to this could be that she knew she had been stupid to allow herself to become vulnerable in this way and that she was abnormal in allowing herself to continue in this relationship. Help was offered when she acknowledged the real cause of the problem, but she refused further aid.

After an event such as this, it is easy to be judgemental because someone did not accept our help. It should not influence your future altitude to people in similar situations. We should not overlook the possibility that this girl did indeed make changes because we were able to help her focus on her real predicament.

It is worth remembering that because you have been faced with the strong feelings of one single, sordid, violent incident, you have not become an expert about all such incidents. The one incident, however, can be such a disturbing experience for the nurse, that she will resist involvement in future cases. One nurse I spoke to in the USA described her 2 years in crisis work with rape and sexual abuse patients. She described how she needed to be alert to the way it could change her views on men and relationships, and how this kind of work could damage the worker. Staff involved in these crises need to have time to discuss and share the intense feelings that arise from their work.

The crisis of rape and sexual abuse

If you return to the observations in Chapter 1 about what happens to individuals in crisis, it will help with your evaluation of the patient who has been raped.

The patient may be criticised about the way she acts and speaks about the incident — the crisis produces a disjointed response and inconsistencies. There may be confusion about the events and time intervals. The tension and restlessness may be interspersed with periods of crying and sobbing, and swings between indifference and flippant remarks. The extreme anger and its accompanying choice of words may be quite disturbing.

It would be easy to criticise her for the way she acts or behaves. It should not be surprising that rape produces strong feelings and disequilibrium, which in turn create responses which are difficult to understand. It is all too easy to label them as being inappropriate for the situation.

Try to be aware of your own feelings and the way they influence your care. You may be confronted with the possibility that you or a close friend or relative could be raped, and how would you cope? This is an issue we would rather not think about, and we may transfer this to the care of our patient.

CRIMINAL VIOLENCE AGAINST THE ELDERLY AND OTHERS

In any close relationship there will be conflict and misunderstanding and feelings of hostility. We should not close our eyes to the fact that elderly couples assault each other physically and mentally, and abuse each other as any other 'couples' do. The guidelines previously discussed about violence in relationships apply equally to the elderly.

The most familiar form violence against the elderly is when they are victims of crime. It is a sad reflection on our society that mugging and robbery with violence are on the increase, and the elderly are the most vulnerable targets. Some will die from the injuries or the consequences of them. The lives of others will be changed dramatically, as they are afraid to live by themselves and no longer feel safe in their own community.

The all-embracing implication of violence against the elderly is that their families are faced with a real crisis. Various members of the family may be asked to care for the victim permanently. This can involve accommodation problems — someone giving up their bedroom; change of lifestyle — giving up work to devote time to caring for elderly relative; infrigement of personal privacy — discussing commitment to the patient with health care staff. This can produce hostility and estrangement within families, and unresolved conflict and disarray can then re-emerge. In the midst of this is the patient/victim, feeling responsible for it all. As I have demonstrated before (Wright 1985) much help will be needed with establishing the focus of the problem and dealing with the immediate situation.

Victims of criminal violence

People can be robbed in shops or at work. Violent attack may be an occupational hazard as in the case of police and security officers, and, although an attack is an acknowledged possibility, when it happens it is still perceived as a crisis.

There are specific guidelines which must be followed for the immediate hospital care of victims of violent attacks. These help us to use the time we have with the patient more effectively, and remind us that the physical and psychological care go together:

1. Bloodstained clothing should be removed and the patient cleaned up as soon as possible. The retention of these items reinforces the contamination felt. The lift in mood, when relatives arrive with fresh clean clothing, is most apparent.

2. When police officers are involved, allow them access to the patient as soon as is practically possible. This helps the victim to offer something positive to help catch the attacker and to redeem the situation they are in. At the same time, being interviewed by the police is quite daunting for some people and can cause the innocent to feel guilty and ashamed. Give them privacy if possible.

3. Undress the patient carefully, and use this time to encourage him to talk. He may not volunteer information about injuries if he becomes withdrawn and sad. It will need your skilful observation to detect some injuries. You will be looking for poor range of movement in limbs and signs of swelling and bruising.

4. Encourage him to discharge feelings about himself and his attacker. You may hear strong emotions being expressed, or generalisations about the patient's future life. He may feel

this incident influences his whole future and the outcome of any plans he had. Do not simply dismiss these statements because they reveal how strongly the patient feels. Taking note of these feelings and working with them is useful and may encourage their discharge.

5. The contact between you and the patient, both physical and emotional, will help to bring him back to reality. If the transaction with you is warm and caring, it will help to dispel the idea that all mankind is like the attacker. Some initial mistrust and hostility on his part may be explained by reaction to the attack.

6. Avoid judgemental remarks about why the attack occurred. You may say, or imply by your behaviour, that the victim was in some way to blame for this situation. Although an evaluation of why the attack occurred can be useful, this is not the time for that.

7. A mild sedative/tranquillizer may be prescribed by the patient's doctor for a few days, to help deal with any sleep disturbances — sleeplessness or nightmares — induced by the attack. Others believe that these should remain painfully apparent in order to allow a useful focusing and discharge of fear and anxiety.

8. Some patients will benefit from follow-up later by a victim support group, the GP, community psychiatric nurse or a social worker. This applies particularly to the socially isolated, the elderly and the family in crisis. The elderly and infirm feel particularly vulnerable both physically and psychologically.

ROAD TRAFFIC AND OTHER ACCIDENTS

Between the ages of 4 and 44 years, we are more likely to die as a result of a road traffic accident than from any other cause. Every year 20 000 motor cyclists will die from injuries sustained in this way, and one in three fatalities in road traffic accidents will be pedestrians. All these statistics relate to deaths. Many thousands more will suffer serious and, in some cases, multiple injuries. Many hours will be spent by police officers and insurance company personnel investigating and discussing who was at fault.

Some of the awful consequences are avoided in the immediate situation by focusing on where the blame lies, and the answer to this question may determine for the patient whether he is the victim of himself or of others. If he is the victim of himself, a crisis may occur due to his preoccupation with the overall damage his behaviour has had on himself and on many other people. Because he think he 'deserves to be punished' he may sabotage treatment subconsciously, or be unco-operative. To him, it may be more acceptable if he is unpopular and disliked, because this is what he deserves. In others you will see the responses we have already discussed — apathy and withdrawal.

Imagine, if you can, finding yourself being totally dependent on others — needing to trust complete strangers with vital decisions and for your every need. Your normal, everyday life suddenly becomes totally disrupted. You are helpless and dependent, and hear conversations about yourself which cause you great distress. You believe that these people can act in ways that determine whether you live or die.

Mattison (1975) discusses the value of reducing anxiety right from the start, including the rescue and emergency department treatment. Efforts which reduce anxiety and promote courage and inner resources during the critical phase of the ordeal will help with the problems of the reality and will promote earlier psychological recovery. This idea discounts the often-made suggestion that patients who are physiologically shocked are usually unaware of surroundings and full impact of what is happening.

Mattison also demonstrates the way in which many psychoses and neuroses can be traced to bodily trauma. Although these studies can make observations on the outcome of patients' failing to cope with trauma, they provide no evidence as to why others are able to cope psychologically.

Morkovin (1982) describes the first phase for trauma victims as being *denial*:

'This can't be happening to me.'

Then *fear* takes over:

'Don't leave me. Am I going to die?'

This fear is about the immediate and later chance of a recurrence of the trauma.

Morkovin describes *anger* as the healthiest response, but this may be repressed because of guilt. She suggests that this repression produces apathy and indifference to the outcome of the injuries.

Finally comes *resolution*, which should occur eventually, and observations should be made to see that this stage has been reached.

Some problems which can occur are flashbacks, difficulty with concentration, nightmares and sleep disturbance. Psychosomatic symptoms are very common. Once you have established communication with the traumatised victim the following guidelines may be of help:

1. Tell the patient where he is and what is happening. Touch his hand or face to confirm that you are real and present and that the voice belongs to you. This will reassure him and help to establish the reality and deal with the fear.

2. If he is able to speak, ask what happened. Provide feedback so he knows that you understand. Validate the feelings associated with the experience.

3. If you can, involve the patient in decisions about his care. Tell him what you are doing and confirm that it is important to you to know how he feels and what he thinks. This will help him return to the belief he has some control over what happens to him, and will remove the child-like dependence.

4. Avoid leaving the patient alone in the acute stage. Until his family arrives, the feeling of total isolation is very strong.

5. Avoid reinforcing the patient's feelings of guilt or self blame. Remember the importance of management in the acute phase.

Schnaper et al (1976) reported observations they made on an intensive care unit, comparing cardiac surgery patients and multiple trauma victims. The main difference is that the cardiac patients had mobilised their defences prior to surgery, and multiple trauma victims had obviously not. The task with the trauma victims, therefore, was to help them locate resources within themselves.

The removal from the scene, and reception into hospital, of a patient with multiple injuries, require immediate and definite responses. The sense of urgency, the raised voices and aggressive response as clothes are cut away can produce humiliation and fear and total vulnerability. The psychological care begins at the scene of the incident, and somehow has to be part of that urgent and often apparently chaotic resuscitation activity.

VIOLATED BY THE SYSTEM

Some patients are victims of political systems and they arrive for care more disadvantaged than others. They are in the terrible position of being unable to protest at indignity or to discharge disruptive feelings of hostility. We should be aware, not only of different cultural responses, but of how people who are suppressed or violated by various political regimes will have even greater difficulty in locating feelings.

Ann Hargreaves (1983), as a nurse and fact-finding delegate to El Salvador, described how the country's health care system was in total disarray, with evidence of tortures, beatings and murders. She found that the human rights violations ran so deep in El Salvador that people were stripped of the basic elements essential for physical and psychological survival.

Patients who have survived concentration camps will describe how long-term suppression of crisis produces psychosis, and how some were helped to discharge strong feelings frequently and in safety. Where patients are from different cultures or politically suppressive régimes, a rapport may be required which includes giving the patient permission to verbalize negative feelings.

Our knowledge of the victim has, by necessity, increased over the last few years, and we have some insight into how people maintain or restore equilibrium when victimised. For some, being victimized by the employment scene or class system produces hostile responses. Some patients will feel victimized by the health care system itself and we perceive them as being difficult or awkward. We will return to this topic later in the chapter about the difficult patient.

QUESTIONS FOR DISCUSSION

1. Discuss the feelings and associated responses you may be confronted with in the victim of a violent attack.
2. Discuss how our rapport with the patient/victim is damaged by our judgemental response.

REFERENCES

Dixon T, Lucas M 1982 The human race. Methuen, London
Eysenck H J i979 The origins of violence. Journal of Medical Ethics
    5: 105–107
Geis G 1982 The framework of violence. In: Warner C, Brain E (eds) Topics
    in emergency medicine 3:4. Aspen Publications, Gartiersburg, Maryland,
    USA
Hargreaves A 1983 Special report of health care in El Salvador. Nursing
    Outlook 131:4
Hight D W, Bakalar H R, Lloyd J R 1979 Journal of the American Medical
    Association 242: 517–520
Mattison E I 1975 Psychological aspects of severe physical injury and its
    treatment. Journal of Trauma 15:3
Morkovin V 1982 Care of the injured patient's emotional trauma. In: Wilson
    D H, Marsden A K (eds) Care of the acutely ill and injured. London
Onions C T (ed) 1983 The shorter Oxford english dictionary. Oxford
    University Press, Oxford
Orr J 1984 Violence against women. Nursing Times 80:17
Rounsaville B J 1978 Battered wives: Barriers to identification and treatment.
    American Journal of Orthopsychiatry 48(3): 487–494
Russell C, Russell W M S 1979 The natural history of violence. Journal of
    Medical Ethics 5: 108–117
Schnaper N, Cowley R, Adams 1976 Overview: psychiatric sequelae to
    multiple trauma. American Journal of Psychiatry 133:8
Stark E, Flitcraft A, Grem A, Robinson J 1979 Psychiatric perspectives on the
    abuse of women: A critical approach. Yale University Centre for Health
    Studies
Tokarski P 1982 Management of child abuse. In: Warner C, Brain G R (eds)
    Topics in emergency medicine 3:4
Treherne J 1984 The strange history of Bonnie and Clyde. Cape, London
Wright B 1981 The victims of violence. Nursing Times 177:47
Wright B 1983 Who are the regulars? Nursing Times 179:7
Wright B 1985 Psychiatric nurse clinicians in emergency areas. In: Altschul
    A T (ed) Psychiatric nursing. Recent Advances in Nursing Series.
    Churchill Livingstone, Edinburgh

7

Disasters

There is no standard definition of a disaster or major accident. One useful way of trying to define it is to look at resources and responses. An incident, accident or disaster that requires special arrangements because of the number of live casualties, and because the usual resources cannot cope unaided, can be classified as a disaster. If the Emergency Department is empty, the staff there may cope with 10 patients with multiple injuries. If the Department is full, and they have cases of two cardiac arrests and three multiple injuries amongst their patients, another 10 could mean a doubling of the numbers of the staff.

Major accidents vary in their nature and severity. Floods, fires, nuclear accidents, chemical spills, explosions and traffic accidents all produce certain types of medical and social emergencies. Most of these incidents are unexpected and out of our control. Others are perceived as disasters when we are confronted with a problem the enormity of which people suddenly become aware, such as a famine. More difficult psychological problems occur in situations where a potential hazard suddenly produces death and destruction. The strength of hostile feelings, associated with being ignored by the government or authorities, can produce long-term disturbance. Some disasters result in few casualties but hold

119

a potential hazard for the population. These, then, by their nature, become health care problems.

Hargreaves (1979) describes how a blizzard prevented patients from returning home from hospital, staff getting to work or back home, and how patients in the community were vulnerable because pharmacies failed to open and patients were deprived of community support. This snow produced a crisis for many separated, isolated, frail and vulnerable people. The panic it produced in people turned them into patients, and those who were already patients needed help with panic as well.

Major hospitals and local authorities will have plans for responding to major incidents and disasters. Our own Department of Health and Social Security has guidelines for making arrangements to deal with major accidents (DHSS 1977). One striking omission from many of these plans concerns guidelines for teaching, training or the actual handling of the emotional crisis produced by these incidents. There are three reasons why we need to plan for this:

1. Not only will victims experience crisis associated with the disaster, but many friends and relatives may arrive and respond in a similar way. Therefore, although we may be able to assess potential injuries fairly quickly, the potential for emotionally difficult and disruptive reactions in people is much greater. We have no choice but to respond to them when faced with them.

2. To be effective in our management of the crisis, we need training and teaching, and a successful way of doing this is in workshops. The provision of training will reduce stress and burn-out in the workers.

3. In our role in preventive medicine, crisis counselling will reduce long-term emotional and physical problems. Bennett (1970) reports the development of physical and psychological problems following serious floods in Bristol. Apart from deaths and illnesses as a direct result of this flood, there was an increase in both physical and psychological problems in the aftermath. Erikson (1976) reported an increase in juvenile delinquency and alcohol and drug abuse after the Buffalo Creek Disaster.

It is therefore important to intervene effectively at the onset of the crisis.

THE INDIVIDUAL AND COMMUNITY RESPONSE

Although there are many slight variations, most researchers' concepts of the stages of response to disaster fit in with Tyhurst's observations (1951). This framework of stages was developed over 30 years ago but remains useful today, and others have built around it. Tyhurst describes three phases:

1. the period of impact
2. recoil
3. post-traumatic period.

Kaffrissen et al (1975) explore separately the period of alarm and threat prior to these three phases. Some disasters involve a sudden, unexpected onset as with an explosion or a flash flood, whereas in other situations a disaster is known to be approaching, as with a tornado or rising flood water. The potential threat produces heightened anxiety and increasing fear and apprehension. This period of alarm may be useful in that it will drive most people to prepare for impact and gather together resources. Some, however, may exhibit atypical behaviour here.

The period of threat is an urgent warning of immediate danger. The individual must decide whether to act or not and to make a decision as to whether his life is threatened. Physical safety will not be the sole reason for motivating a person to find a safe place. He will ask what the physical, emotional and material costs of escape are. It is when faced with these decisions that he has to evaluate his life, relationships and property, the threatened loss of which may produce a crisis.

Hargreaves (1980) in a further paper on coping with disaster, demonstrates that after the three phases described by Tyhurst in 1951, there is a period of complaining about the agencies connected with the disaster management and relief.

Panic is not as common as you would believe. It is associated with lack of leadership, belief that escape routes are closing and immediate severe danger. Preventive measures and controls need to be strictly enforced to prevent this.

STAGES OF RESPONSE

1. Impact

Behaviour at this stage is disorganised and there is less likely to be response to directions. The victims are stunned, dazed and apathetic and this can last for minutes or hours. Tyhurst estimates that between 10 and 25% remain cool and collected during this phase, and the majority of the rest acts stunned. He describes them as reporting lack of feeling or emotion, and behaving in a zombie-like manner. Only a small group, (about 10–15%) behave as you see demonstrated by the media in disaster situations, i.e. screaming, crying, becoming paralysed or confused. The responses we have discussed in other crises will be evident — tension, disorganization, hopelessness and agitation.

2. Recoil

In this period the initial stresses have ceased or the individual has escaped them. There is a gradual awareness of what has happened and a return of emotional expression. There will be a great need for victims to be with others, to discharge feelings, and there will be gratitude for help. They may minimise their own injuries and be very altruistic, asking that others be helped first. It is said that, at this stage, they are more open to suggestion and perhaps they are more accessible. These signs suggest that you may begin some purposeful intervention at this stage. Some people will feel guilty simply because they have survived.

3. Post-traumatic stage

This can be the longest in duration of the stages of response. For some, emotional crisis will occur 6 months later. At the start of the post-traumatic stage there is a heightened morale and a feeling of brotherhood and identification with the community at large. Some euphoria may be seen, as plans are made for the future. During this period, dreams and night-mares occur, as the victim comes to a full realisation of what the disaster meant in terms of loss and bereavement.

Singer (1982) in his paper on considerations of a psychologi cal nature in disaster, returns to three considerations which are well-known to you by now — anger, guilt and defensive reactions. These three factors play a major part in many crises, and they remain significant in disaster crisis counselling.

ANGER

It is common for disaster victims to feel angry, which is understandable as it seems an appropriate response to being threatened and hurt. Less understandable is the fact that the anger is often directed at areas of pre-existing conflicts, or other targets such as minority groups, the financially successful, civic officials and the government. Occasionally the anger is justified as the blame will lie with one of these but more often it is scapegoating. There is a great need to offload the blame and to begin to accuse. This outpouring sounds like a safety valve.

GUILT

This is often expressed very powerfully and with great distress. Survivors ask themselves whether they could have done more to save people's lives or alleviate suffering. Others, as we have said, will simply feel guilty that they survived when others died. They may say that others deserved to live and they themselves did not. You will hear this response after a sudden death, but when the guilt has a more supernatural element to it, this can be more difficult to confront. An example of this is where a couple have an argu-ment, and one wishes the other dead. When one dies in a disaster, the other feels in some way responsible. On a rational and intellectual level the person knows he has no power over such incidents, but he punishes himself with the thought that he has.

DEFENSIVE REACTIONS

Denial of the reality of what is happening all around them is a common reaction.

'Please wake me up and tell me it's dream.'
'You have the wrong person. I don't belong in this story.'

You will hear others talk of 'gallows humour' as an effective defence mechanism. Intellectualising about some trivial aspect of the incident is a way of avoiding the painful focus. Hysterical conversion symptoms, which include deafness blindness and paralysis, have been reported.

'Am I going mad?' is a question I have been asked in crisis situations which indicates how overwhelmed people are. It should be stressed at this stage that these responses to major accidents and disasters are quite normal. They do not mean the clients or patients are psychiatrically ill. Indeed, it may well cause you some concern if an individual shows *no* sign of distress — the problem here is that this may produce maladaptive methods of coping with the crisis, such as denial. The crisis may bring into play old material, and introduce the difficulty of where to focus the coping mechanisms. The task of the crisis worker is to encourage and help locate good coping mechanisms.

Much of the work on the management of crisis in disasters stems from Lindemann's classic paper (1944) on acute crisis following the Coconut Grove Fire. This paper presented the fundamentals of crisis theory as a conceptual framework for preventive psychiatry. Since then, others have documented the type of intervention or psychological first aid that is useful. Due to the overwhelming nature of disaster, it is necessary to work within some guidelines, in order to help prevent feelings of being swamped and in a state of panic.

The following points may be a useful reminder and are referred to in the case study on pages 129–136.

THE DISASTER VICTIM IN CRISIS

1. You will be confronted by an individual suffering from physical, psychological and social problems, but your focus

will be directed to caring for the person *you* are faced with — he will need care and support with his *immediate* feelings and problems. If you attempt to take on more, you and your client may be overwhelmed by the enormity of the problems. It is the immediate feelings that incapacitate. Mechanisms to cope with these, will allow the client to move on and face his other problems.

2. Obtain and share accurate information about the incident and the victims. Witholding information for long periods will produce hostility and cause you more problems. Make stringent efforts to check the accuracy of the information — it is not useful to pass on rumours. Keeping accurate records, and having a central co-ordinating point for the information, will be reassuring to relatives. If they have to trek from one place to another to get accurate information, they will begin to doubt your efficiency in the care of the patient. This would add more anxiety to an already traumatic situation.

3. As soon as it is practical, allow a relative to see the patient or the body. I have heard the anguish of not knowing for sure whether it is their loved one be described as torment and agony. The patient will be reassured if he knows he is not alone, and his anxiety will be reduced. It will make the task of caring for the family easier. The confirmation will then allow them to do something — there is a great need to 'do something' in order to relieve agitation. This confirmation will also also allow them to go to inform other key people, and to concentrate on comforting each other. Once relatives have all the necessary information as to the medical care and the prognosis, it allows them to act on a practical level. Often you will have heard:

'Now we know, we can make arrangements for the children . . .' (or care of other members of the family).

4. Families, neighbours and communities displaced by a disaster will benefit from being brought together. If possible, arrange care within that community because to be move too far away will emphasise the loss. With members of the family scattered around a large hospital or hospitals, a co-ordinator can facilitate a family reunion.

5. The management of the crisis needs skilled personnel. People need explanations about why they respond as they do,

that their response is appropriate and that it does not mean they are going mad.

6. Give no false assurances about the severity of the incident; instead, help to confront the reality. This is painful for both the giver and receiver of the information, but there is no way to avoid it. By being honest and confronting it, you do nothing that will produce mistrust in your relationship with these people. You are prepared, after imparting such information, to give comfort and care.

At this stage, be cautious about relatives persuading you that a loved one needs sedation. Individuals usually resist and rarely ask for it. In contrast, relatives often feel it will be best for the patient, when in reality is is to help the relatives to cope with situation. They would rather see a loved one sedated than suffering.

7. Your contact with these people is limited. Discourage dependency but work towards their responding in ways which will resolve the crisis. Remember the disorganisation that occurs and help them towards meaningful activity. They will begin to see some order in the chaos. This is encouraging when faced with overwhelming disintegration.

8. Identify and use the leaders and resourceful people from the family and community. Remember your transaction is limited.

To summarize

1. Remember your limitations.
2. Disseminate information accurately.
3. Lessen anxiety by allowing contact between patient and family.
4. Facilitate family and community support.
5. Crisis intervention gives information, and requires skill.
6. There are things you cannot avoid. You need to be honest, even though this is distressing for you both.
7. Permit limited dependency.
8. Use community/family resources.

SUPPORT FOR THE WORKERS

Someone who is directing operations should be responsible for arranging rest periods and for providing refreshments for rescue workers. Workers need to be reassured during this very stressful work that someone cares for them. The director of operations should be aware of the areas of work that are more harrowing or stressful, in order to arrange more rest periods here.

The staff in the hospital will need reminding about their response to the rescue workers. Ambulance personnel, for example, may have worked very hard to resuscitate a patient, carried him over difficult terrain and have been in danger themselves. They may have invested a lot in the care of that patient, and when they hand him over to the nursing staff in the hospital, they do not immediately lose interest in him and will value information later as to his condition. We are often remiss by failing to say to them what a good job they have done, or failing to pass information back to them later, or by dismissing them quickly.

In work on stress by Sanner (1983) the stressful responses of workers during simulated military disasters were described. Although these disasters were simulated in order to evaluate efficiency of personnel, many participants were distressed if their mock patients were declared dead. Others were made deeply aware of how stressful the real work would be. They were able to use their observations to increase the amount of training to give support for the stresses of the work. They were also better prepared for these stresses and for psychological problems that occur in the aftermath of disasters.

Those of you who have worked in Emergency Departments will be aware of the staff's need to talk after prolonged resuscitation periods, especially if it was a particularly bloody and messy incident. In planning for major incidents, adequate space for refreshments and recreation of staff is a necessity. It will answer some of the immediate psychological needs of wanting to talk about the incident and to discharge strong feelings about it. It is also a place that confirms the support and warmth you share with your colleagues, where you have the luxury of time to enquire of a colleague's well — being if you know he has have had a particularly difficult time. This refreshment/sitting room becomes an extremely important place.

One sign that a worker is having some difficulty coping with stress will be if he begins to display the reactions of the disaster victims. Irritability, fault finding, unreasonable criticism of the authorities and the management of the disaster may be the first signs. Imagining that he is being displaced by other members of the team may indicate how vulnerable he feels. You should also be aware that some workers will identify more with certain victims. For example, a bus full of schoolchildren from a major accident will cause more problems for the mothers on the staff.

The people involved in post-disaster evaluation, at say 1–2 weeks later, may reveal evidence of staff who had difficulty. This post-disaster evaluation usually shows up some deficiencies in planning or organisation, and it also highlights usefully the stressful areas of activity. It may also disclose who needs more training in coping with stress, and it will certainly serve as a reminder to management that the training to handle stress is important.

PLANNING FOR MAJOR ACCIDENT AND DISASTER

The immediate and long-term psychological care of disaster victims needs to be part of our disaster plans. There are now many documented experiences of disaster that support this, but it continues to be omitted or given little consideration. The Minneapolis St Paul International Airport Disaster Plan (Butcher 1980) includes definite provision for the psychological care of passengers surviving an air crash, and also of their relatives and friends.

Nurses have to make rapid decisions about the care of patients and relatives, and making these decisions, when being bombarded from all sides with other requests is stressful. How we handle this, and what makes us more efficient or less so in these situations, needs teaching. Arranging training in workshops, with some theory and role play, is perhaps the best way to teach these skills. Nurses and other staff will need to be taught Crisis Intervention and other ways to give psychological care and support in disaster situations.

This will help them to be more effective and therefore more efficient.

From the victim's point of view, your appropriate response to his crisis will promote his recovery. Longmire (1984) demonstrated how, after Hurricane Frederick struck the Gulf coasts of Mississippi and Alabama, there was a dramatic increase in the number of patients seen immediately and for 2 weeks after. Although some of these were trauma patients, there was also an increase in those needing obstetrical and psychiatric support. The improved immediate management of the incident can prevent long-term repercussions of the community.

The techniques of crisis intervention have been judged appropriate and successful in dealing with the emotional response to disaster and major accident.

Case study

There was nothing new about pop concerts being held in the city centre exhibition hall. The only change in recent years was that the age of those attending tended to be younger: 12-, 13- and 14-year-olds now made up a large part of the 15 000 audience. What was even more surprising was that some youngsters travelled up to 100 miles without parental supervision. Coach loads arrived from youth cliubs; other large numbers arrived by rail. Past experience determined that some would lose contact with friends, and be frightened and distressed. Others would miss the last bus or train home, and parents would have to be contacted and asked to arrange their transport home.

The local Accident and Emergency Department also knew from past experience that they would probably receive no more than 10 patients. Some of the girls would have fainted with excitement, others would have lost a shoe in the crush and had toes stepped on.

During the evening of this concert, the staff discussed what it would be like to be young again, and reminisced about the stars they had been infatuated with. Some bemoaned the lack of parental supervision and how it was not like that in their day.

The concert was a huge success. The thoughts of some fans

were centred around which door the group would leave by, and whether there was the chance of an autograph. Although some saw how unrealistic this was, others were swept away by the magic of the occasion. When the final curtain came down, rumours had turned into certainties as to where the group would leave from.

In a desperate attempt to get to this spot there was a mad scramble for the doors. The wooden raised steps and gangway trembled and moved dangerously as those at the front struggled to open the emergency doors. Others, aware of the danger, pushed into the crowd as if to add their strength to the opening of the doors. As the steps collapsed, panic, screams and general noise erupted. A large number started to run in the opposite direction to escape the disaster and were crushed.

As the press, television and radio were giving coverage of the event, details were soon appearing on news bulletins. Some parents had rung the hospital before the first patients had arrived.

> *Remind staff about the importance of accurate record keeping for information purposes.*

Peggy, the senior Sister in the Emergency Department, had instituted the Major Accident Procedure on being informed of the disaster by ambulance control. Because of the media coverage and immediate public disclosure of the incident, many staff members and helpers arrived quickly. The more senior and experienced nurses in the Department were allocated to the trauma area.

> *Have definite procedures and policies about who goes where.*

Ambulance control gave the information that 10–15 youngsters would arrive shortly with serious multiple injuries. The nurses for the trauma area, and the triage nurses, were informed of this.

One of the resuscitation nurses began to get agitated, asking where everyone was to go, and saying she had always said the Department was too small.

Reassure her and remind her of where her focus is. Keep within your boundaries.

All the outside telephone lines to the Department were blocked by anxious parents. Some had arrived and were demanding information. A porter came through and said he had heard there were at least 200 casualties.

Warn about spreading rumours or acting upon them.

Jenny, a 14-year-old with two broken legs, was obviously in pain as she was undressed. She wept bitterly about the distress she was causing her mother, who lived 50 miles away. Angrily, she blamed her peers for their behaviour.

Encourage discharge of feelings.

But she quickly returned to the fact that she had made a complete mess of things. Her guilty feelings about her mother were too much for the staff who told her:
'You should not feel like that.'
'It's not your fault.'
'Don't be silly, how can it be?'

Do not invalidate the patient's feelings, but work with them.

The parents of a 15-year-old boy were being told by the Registrar and Charge Nurse that their son had just died from serious chest injuries. As they held each other's hands tightly it was explained how the boy had died despite intensive measures to save him. Both parents expressed disbelief and could only repeat that it must be a mistake.

Refer to Chapter 3 on sudden death to prepare yourself for some difficult responses.

It was explained that it would be necessary to identify the body in the presence of a police officer.
'We will leave you alone together with your son,' the nurse explained,' as you will probably want to spend some time with him. Some people value this later.'

This gives them permission to spend some time with the deceased. They may have felt unable to ask about this, because the department is busy.

This identification also helped with their feelings of unreality.

A crowd of people at the reception desk was becoming increasingly hostile about the lack of information regarding numbers and names.

Other members of the team also feel stress.

The clerk needed support in her stressful role, and had little or no information:

Update your information at regular intervals.

There were now 43 patients in the Department, 19 with severe multiple injuries. At a notice board giving details of where the patients were located a nurse sat re-evaluating priorities and supporting nurses who did not normally work in the Department. She provided information about types of dressings and their location, and equipment needed. As she was being bombarded with questions from all sides, the senior nurse supervising this area handed over the role of location of patients to another nurse to lighten the load.

The decisions you make are not definitive. Re-evaluate and change them if necessary.

The newly-assigned nurse was able to reunite some less seriously injured patients with their families while they waited for doctors. This also removed some of the pressure from the reception clerks.

Remember Point 3 (p. 125): Separation produces stress and problems for you and the family.

Large groups of people other than relatives began to arrive. Civic leaders, volunteers, friends and neighbours of the families. The catering supervisor had arranged for tea, and a place was set aside for people to talk, thereby encouraging support and camaraderie.

This area can be the point to meet or for finding people.

A middle-aged lady who had recently been widowed was told that her daughter was in the operating theatre having surgery for severe head injuries. She screamed out loud at the news, and called the doctor a liar when she was informed that her daughter might not recover fully. The anger was difficult for the doctor and nurse to cope with, as it seemed to accuse them of incompetence. The woman then cried bitterly, and when alone with the nurse later, asked her if she thought she was mad. *The nurse was able to explain to her what happens to people in these crises.*

Point 5 (p. 125): The management of crisis needs skilled personnel.

The woman's eyes begged for some news that would lighten the awful burden and distress. The nurse remembered how easy it would be to avoid the real problem by giving false assurances:

Point 6 (p. 126): Facing the reality is painful but should not be avoided.

As two members of the pop group, and more members of the media arrived, the reception area became more chaotic. Television cameras were brought in, trailing long cables, and relatives were being interviewed.

Use security to help to control the media.

The extra personnel, visitors and activity added to the chaotic scene.

Administrators were used to attempt to put some order and control into the situation.

Disorder and lack of control add to the individual's confusion. It will help control the feeling of disorder experienced by people if the Department runs smoothly and calmly.

On the other hand, by virtue of the size of the disaster, things do not run like clockwork at these times.

Amy was working in the resuscitation room. She had been a staff nurse in Emergency for 1 year, and had experienced resuscitation of multiple injuries. Her patient, a 13-year-old girl, needed the attention of many disciplines. The neurosurgeons were assessing her fractured base of skull, and peritoneal lavage was being performed by the surgeons to evaluate her abdominal trauma. In assessing these priorities, each doctor felt his own area to be the highest priority. Amy became aware of how irritable and hostile they were becoming.

> *Circulating nurse or supervisor now aware of signs of stress.*

The urinary catheterisation somehow became difficult, and Amy twice compromised the aseptic technique and began again.

All the time, Amy was aware that the central venous pressure line looked precarious. The IV line into the girl's left arm was about to run through. In her haste to return quickly with the ice, Amy dropped it. Why couldn't she find the subclavian catheter? She had used it many times. She knew the Department like the back of her hand.

'Yes, I heard you,' she thought, pulling boxes out as she searched for the Heimlich valve. 'I have never liked that surgeon,' she told herself, suddenly ashamed at being tearful and out of control.

> *Do not wait until it is too late. Try to be aware of excessive stress.*

Sheila arrived suddenly, and told Amy it was her turn to get the coffee, and asked for an update on the patient's condition. She also gave the surgeon a disapproving look, and as Amy scurried out, he thanked her for her help.

The staff sitting room was alive with conversation, and everyone was able to get up to date with the whole picture.

A place, separate but easily accessible from the main department, is high on the list of needs for staff.

The nursing officer arrived with the total casualty figures, and said they had now received the last patient from the scene and everything was under control.

Information is also important for staff.

This helped them all to grasp the entire situation and how they fitted into it.

Hours later many groups of anxious relatives were still coming and going. Some left looking relieved and happy, while others left distraught and requiring support.

Before the staff withdrew and relaxed too much, all equipment was replaced and checked.

A state of continual readiness is essential.

That night there would be a strong need for the staff to discuss what had happened. In 2 or 3 days, a more objective evaluation of the whole management of the disaster would be necessary. This would not only high-light weaknesses, but the written evaluation could be used to show strengths and give praise where necessary. A continuous training of staff and updating of equipment is an absolute must.

Training and retraining — an ongoing process.

One family, leaving at dawn, returned to say thankyou to a nurse who had cared for them. As Owen's mother put her arms round the nurse to thank her for her love and care, she told the nurse that Owen had died half an hour previously. Both cried openly. Later, the nurse said she felt there was nothing to stop her crying, which made her supervisor feel good. The others knew that she, too, had shed a few tears for them.

Fire, flood, war, railways, planes and cars all produce

disasters at times. Famine, disease and earthquake are some of the disasters that do not affect civilisation as commonly, but they are still disasters. Some are unexplained, and in insurance terms are 'Acts of God'. Others are due to man's inhumanity to man, or his carelessness or neglect.

Keep aware of trends, and of special occasions when large crowds could gather. Some areas have particular hazards — mines, chemicals, radiation be aware of them.

Whatever the cause, the loss and devastation touch families and individuals, and are a unique and special experience for them. The pain and distress will take many forms and it is to these individuals we will respond. They will require our care, love and support. But although these are powerful responses, they are not enough, for in the midst of the chaos and disorder we can usefully intervene and our skills can allow the individual to re-emerge. It is so easy to feel at a loss when faced with these individuals, but you do not have to feel this way.

QUESTIONS FOR DISCUSSION

1. Discuss how to introduce some order into the chaotic situation of a disaster.
2. Discuss lines of communication at the hospital — why are these important?

REFERENCES

Bennett E 1970 Bristol floods 1968. Controlled survey of effects on health of local community disasters. British Medical Journal 3: 454–458
Butcher J N 1980 The role of crisis intervention on an airport disaster plan. Aviation, Space and Environmental Medicine 51: 1260–1262
Department of Health and Social Security 1977 HC (1977) 1 dealing with major accidents. DMSS, London
Erikson K T 1976 Loss of communality at Buffalo Creek. American Journal of Psychiatry 3: 302–305
Hargreaves A 1979 et al Blizzard 78: Dealing with disaster. American Journal of Nursing 79: 268–271
Hargreaves A 1980 Coping with disaster. American Journal of Nursing 91:683

Kaffrissen S R, Heffron E F, Zusman J 1975 Mental health problems in environmental disasters. Emergency Psychiatric Care. Charles Press, New York

Lindemann E 1974 Symptomatology and management of acute grief. American Journal of Psychiatry 101: 141–148

Longmire A W 1984 Morbidity of hurricane Frederick. Annals of Emergency 13:5

Sanner P H 1983 Stress reactions among participants in mass casualty simulations. Annals of Emergency Medicine 12:7

Singer T J 1982 An introduction to disaster: some considerations of a psychological nature. Aviation, Space and Environmental Medicine, March 1982 245–250

Tyhurst J S 1951 Individual reactions to community disaster American Journal of Psychiatry 107:764

8

The disruptive and difficult patient and his family

When considering the disruptive and difficult patient, I had to decide where to place the focus of attention. Should we concentrate on improving our interaction with the patient or should we begin with the nurse examining her own feelings and reactions? Both of these approaches must play some part. We have our own prejudices and feelings about certain types of patients: some of them appear determined to sabotage what we do despite a clearly non-judgemental approach from us. In some cases it may be clear where the work needs to start, but, in other situations, issues in both areas will have to be considered. Whatever the cause, our task will be to provide an atmosphere where each individual (including the staff) is heard and valued, and where meaningful interaction can take place.

Good interaction may, of course, be grossly undermined or even prevented by the organisation or institution itself. There are many examples of this. Sue Aitken (1984) highlighted one area that may lead to poor relationships:

> The two most powerful professions in the National Health Service — nursing and medicine — are arranged in tight hierarchies whose military origins and ethos are manifest in countless ways. We have duty rosters, nursing and medical officers, going on leave (never anything as self-indulgent as holidays), uniforms to denote rank — hats, belts, pins, badges, epaulettes and so on. An army needs an enemy. In physical

medicine germs and broken bones are clearly the baddies; the person really only exists as a kind of garrison for them.

If the institution or organisation encourages a 'them and us' attitude we will have to look for ways of changing the organisation.

Our own background, class, culture or race may mean that we view some particular patients in good or bad lights. When we were vulnerable student nurses, we may have been influenced to believe that certain types of patients were good or bad. There is clear evidence that nurses do label patients in this way and that their responses are often based on ill-informed assumptions made about these individuals.

In their examination of the nursing role, Kelly & May (1982) discuss how the role of caring nurse needs an appreciative patient. They further state that nurses need the patient to take on a certain role to make sense of their own role. Nurses often need patients to be passive recipients, as this involves an interaction that complements the role of nursing. As the patient is party to this, he has the power to reject the label or the type of help offered. It is at this point that the patient can be labelled unco-operative, disruptive or difficult.

In David Roberts' study (1984) there is a list of the most unpopular patients, at the top of which comes patients who belong to the medical or nursing professions. Is this because they are more likely to reject the label or role suggested? Or is it that, because we identify with them, they remind us of our own vulnerability or mortality? We are likely to be reluctant to admit this, but we should be willing to ask ourselves why.

The other patients featuring prominently on this list are easily predictable: self-poisoning patients, patients with alcohol problems, and patients who do not speak English or who are mentally ill. It is interesting that patients who are terminally ill are more popular with the nurses than are their relatives. Is this because, in their grief, these relatives are more likely to challenge us about our role or care?

Prejudice and dislike are often handed on to other nurses at report time. Many nurses in Roberts' study were able to change their minds after talking to the patient. This would suggest that, although I may try to inluence you to examine your prejudices using an intellectual approach, personal contact is the factor most likely to change your response. Perhaps, then, instead of avoiding certain types of patients, we should increase our contact with them to facilitate change.

Various studies, therefore, highlight the fact that in evaluating the difficult or disruptive patient, we should consider three main areas:

1. The nurse's role

Are we threatened by confrontation about this?

Are we afraid to have our judgement evaluated?

Do the needs of our labelling and care override those of the patient and his perception of his illness?

Are we under some other stress?

2. The patient

Is his behaviour or response an indication of a damaged or difficult personality?

Is he psychiatrically ill?

Is he ill-informed?

Is he being excluded when major decisions are being made about him?

Is there some other factor, such as family or job, which is so disturbing him that he is unable to play his part in his own recovery?

3. The hospital, institution or organisation

Is there some rule or regulation which affects this patient but which overrides his needs?

Are we enforcing some rule or regulation that needs re-evaluating or updating, because of newer information or technology?

Are we enforcing rigidly some outdated philosophy of the organisation, to the detriment of the patient?

These are just some of the questions we can ask ourselves about the areas that influence the care of the patient. In asking them, we may re-evaluate a part of our care that produces conflict between us and the patient. I should also put this the other way round and say between the patient and us — because you will be surprised, if you make a list of causes for complaint, how you were aware of many of them. But being aware does not always mean we act. Indeed many of the complaints we would not want to act upon because they question some fundamental areas of our practice or the organisation. We can easily dismiss them as some strange idea belonging to a difficult person.

AN APPROACH TO THE PROBLEM

In evaluating what produces a difficult patient, it is not always easy to separate him from his family or visitors. Many of you will have had the strong feeling that the difficulty comes from the family or visitor, and it is not at all unusual to hear the remark that certain visitors are best avoided because they are difficult to handle. They may question the quality of medical or nursing care, or complain of not being informed, or the conflict they introduce may simply be between them and the patient. Rather than allow this conflict continually to re-emerge, it is wiser to confront it.

The word 'confrontation' sounds threatening but it does not have to be. A senior nurse on the ward will be involved with the patient, relative or both, in exploring the area that produces the conflict. Statements that give information, or are loaded in some way, can be useful:

'I get the feeling you are dissatisfied or unhappy about something.'

This statement begins by making the point that you are sensitive to the feelings of the patient or relative, which is reassuring to them. As the statement invites them to share feelings, an attempt should be made to offer privacy. If the response covers many problems present and past, then you will have to decide together on the focus, and what you cannot deal with can be referred elsewhere. Your focus will be upon immediate concerns. It may be that anxiety about the illness, injury or prognosis may emerge. Some problems will be dealt with by the medical staff, while others can be resolved by giving information. Many patients and families have unrealistic expectations about care, and again this can be clarified.

Questions concerning the ethics of discussing confidential information about the patient have been dealt with in previous chapters but they remain a cause for concern. Some relatives feel they are entitled to disclosure by virtue of their relationship with the patient. If able, adult patients should be involved in the decision of who should be informed. If the patient is unable to participate and the relative is not particularly close, staff will have to decide whether to disclose information or not. It is clear that you will be faced with a dilemma in some instances, e.g. the case of a 25-year-old man critically ill from an overdose of drugs taken in a suicide attempt. Who do you discuss this with and what do you say? I do not have any easy answer to such a thorny problem and I accept that we often act on feelings we have at the time.

WHEN HOSPITALISATION OFFERS A CHANGE IN STATUS

Some patients or family members will assume or suddenly develop a new status when adjusting to the hospitalisation or illness of themselves or their relative. You will have observed that some people are excited at the drama, suspense and uncertainty which are suddenly introduced into the family. Attempts by staff to reduce the intensity or seriousness of the event are resisted. Subconsciously it may be a welcome break from the routine, or an answer to a problem, or it may be in the interests of the patient or his family to maintain his status of being ill.

For some relatives it offers an opportunity to remind the patient that they will overlook or supervise his care, which will in turn remind him that his family loves and cares for him. You will all be familiar with the relative who demands care for the patient, or information about him. This new-found assertiveness may be possible because of the patient's change in role to the passive and submissive. The dynamics of the family will then be altered and another person can take on his role. In a family group you may have to select the member who is able to receive and disseminate information about the patient. There are times when these situations can be distorted to serve the needs of one member of the family. Most of your patients and families will not respond in a difficult manner, but if they do, these family dynamics should be examined.

The suggestion so far is that there are changes or difficulties within the family that can cause the problems. There will also be difficulties and problems within the health care team and we should not deny this. There must be times when we all have to admit a failure in communication, or in the organisation, and have to apologise for this. A failure to act upon difficulties and hostility may lead to an explosive situation. A storing or building-up of resentment and hostility is to be avoided. Some patient or relatives will be more difficult to handle, or will incapacitate you for some reason. Ask a colleague to help you here; there is no shame in enlisting help when you have to deal with some very difficult person.

A PSYCHOSOMATIC RESPONSE

A psychosomatic disorder is a pathological condition caused by an emotional response. Emotional behaviour refers to extensive and intensive changes in physiological functioning that are psychological in origin. The emotional behaviour is characterised by the physiological functioning of the autonomic effectors. This can include alterations in the heart rate, rate of stomach or duodenal movement and gastric or adrenal gland secretion. Some reactions are sudden or short-lived, and others are prolonged. When it has been decided that a disorder is psychosomatic, the patient still may need prescriptions or other physical intervention or investigation.

When it is suggested that the trouble is all in the patient's mind, some hostility may emerge from him or his family. They may make even more strenuous efforts to convince you that it is not. This can cause even more disruption and a breakdown in rapport between the patient/family and the health care team. Some nurses are at fault here because, after it has been decided the illness has emotional causes, they regard it as no longer their problem. Sticking rigidly to either the biological or the psyhological side is unacceptable, as all biological disorders have psychological elements, and all psychological disorders have biological elements. These two aspects, biological and psychological, must be considered in diagnosis and treatment.

The following are some goals to keep in view when discussing this aspect with the patient or his family:

1. Give information. The patient may not recognise the role of emotions in the development or precipitation of illness. Some examples may be necessary.
2. Help the patient to identify conflicts and situations that produce this response.
3. Assist with suggestions of ways to acquire control over bodily responses to stress. This may mean suggesting less work, holidays, ways of relaxation and possibly even examination of leisure pursuits.
4. Suggest that he sets himself goals to reduce the durations and frequency of physical responses to stress, and to acquire some control over autonomic responses. Your equal concern about this response will show him you recognise its reality — you are not suggesting the patient is mad.

Your responses suggest he has resources and ability to handle this himself, and you do not then devalue the individual or his symptoms. You may need to suggest where he should go for support and guidance with this task.

PANIC ATTACKS

These are characterised by a sudden overwhelming fear, accompanied by a strong physical response. The patient may hyperventilate, develop tetany (spasm of the hands), scream and shout or collapse on the floor. This in turn causes acute anxiety and panic in any witnesses, which can lead to severe disruption. These attacks last for minutes rather than hours, and you are well aware of the patient's fear, which is increased by the spasm of the hands and tingling of the lips and face and fingers.

Your first response here is to give information about the physical manifestations. Explain that hyperventilation produces this tingling and tetany, and encourage slow, deep breathing into a paper bag. To reduce the panic in onlookers, approach the patient calmly and assess methodically his physical condition. Encourage the witnesses to discuss and focus on the occurrence and the feelings it produced in them. Adopt the same approach as for crisis, by working on the immediate problems and keeping within narrow, well-defined boundaries setting limited objectives. By gently discussing how the stimulus produced overwhelming feelings, the patient himself can begin to find mechanisms to control the physical symptoms and to work out a method of approach to the problem.

Situational panic attacks, as seen in the Emergency Department, settle down quickly. This does not mean they are 'hysterical' or unimportant.

SELF-INJURIOUS BEHAVIOUR

Many aspects of this response are covered in Chapter about deliberate self-harm. Patients who mutilate themselves, for example by persistently slashing their wrists, cause severe disruption and distress for other patients and staff. It is with these patients that we associate other acts of violence and disruption. When they arrive with knives, or climb onto the roof or hang from windows threatening to jump, staff must not put themselves in danger. Some of the heroism associated with these incidents is strictly for the television or cinema.

Many of these responses are behavioural disturbances associated with breakdown in communications and families. Many of the people involved have long-term difficulties with relationships. Crisis intervention is therefore not always appropriate. Enlist the help of the police if necessary.

Some of the approaches to communication with the patient in crisis may be useful, but you should ask yourself whether there is anything new or different about this behaviour. Staff involved in this sort of episode need the opportunity to discuss it later, and to have some time to recover from the ordeal. To witness acts of self-mutilation is very distressing and leaves nurses feeling helpless and ineffective.

THE VIOLENT PATIENT

Aggression can become a part of any crisis when strong feelings emerge and individuals are under threat. We may make a quick assessment of the history, premorbid personality and contributing factors such as alcohol, drugs, mental illness or organic confusion. Some of these conditions may help us to decide how long we are going to spend appealing to the individual. Some drugs will impair judgement seriously, and distort the patient's contact with reality, making this approach almost impossible. If others are in danger, we should not hesitate to enlist the help of the police and/or security staff. 'How do we respond when confronted with violence?' is a question asked by many nurses. I think the question should be 'How do we prevent violence from occurring?'

WHY VIOLENCE OCCURS

The usual coping mechanisms break down and the stress within the patient causes him to become restless, agitated and angry. His usual coping method may be to act out this response by behaving aggressively. You may no longer be a person who can help him, but may have become an obstacle preventing him from getting what he wants. What was previously perceived as helpful or useful from you will no longer facilitate an answer. You are witnessing the first signs of approaching violence.

SIGNS THAT VIOLENCE IS DEVELOPING

1. There is a change in his response to your role (see above).
2. He becomes restless, agitated, paces the floor, wrings hands.
3. He demands answers immediately, and appeals for help from others with raised voice.
4. He begins to taunt you and bring you into disrepute. Sacrcasm may be a strong feature.
5. His voice becomes louder or he shouts using obscenities and accusations.

6. You have difficulty in getting his attention, and his iveness begins to show a limited time span.

TACTICS FOR THE PREVENTION OF VIOLENCE

It will be useful to discharge some of the feelings listed above, but not at the expense of others. Other patients within earshot, especially children, the elderly or others who are vulnerable, may fear for their lives. Encourage him to talk about the factors that produced the sudden change, and explain that you find it distressing to see him like this. It may be apparent that he relates better to one specific nurse, or to a doctor. Allow him to do this, but don't leave him alone.

Focus on the immediate problem: try to remember you are dealing with his actions just now, and not with his personality. If you feel you have to take on this aspect of the patient, you may be tempted to give up immediately. It is easy to take remarks and abuse personally, especially if you feel you have invested a lot of your time with this person. Try to control your verbal and non-verbal responses to this sort of feeling — standing defiantly with arms folded, for example, may be interpreted as being aggressive. Maintain eye contact so that he knows he has your attention. Remember it is easy for a smile or a look around the room to be misinterpreted. Do not stand too close as this may be encroaching on his personal space.

IF VIOLENT BEHAVIOUR OCCURS

1. Call for help.
2. Ask fellow members of staff to remove other patients from danger.
3. Try not to get cornered.
4. Avoid threats and raising your voice. Maintain verbal contact.
5. When restraining the patient, use as many people as possible, with one person per limb and two for the body. Do not hurt him, just restrain him.
6. Do not enter into a contract that you cannot keep with him.

Do not offer immunity from the police or prosecution. When police arrive, this will produce more violence.

As an act of violence has now occurred, medical and nursing staff will confer with the police on their arrival. It will have to be decided whether the patient needs medical or nursing intervention, or whether he should be removed. In some cases you will be able to stop restraining him and handle the situation without the police.

It must always be remembered that certain toxic conditions, drug abuse or drug responses, or organic illness may produce violence. Although the police may be involved because someone was in immediate danger, it may not be appropriate to continue to enlist their help. I do not want to give the impression that it is an easy thing to make the decision to use the police or to hand a patient over to them, on the contrary it is often very difficult to decide what to do. Some occasions are easier to deal with than others — the drunk who walks into the Emergency Department is treated for a minor injury, becomes violent and/or refuses to leave. After the medical and nursing staff are satisfied he no longer requires hospital treatment, and the police are called, it is an easy decision to have him removed.

However, there may be another occasion where the drunk, with a large cut and bump on his head, becomes violent. It may be impossible to assess him accurately with a neurological examination because he becomes violent. Can you hand him over to the police without carrying out the assessment? Can he lie in a police cell unobserved for long periods of time.

It is unrealistic of nurses to feel that violence, hostility and aggression are totally alien or unacceptable in patients. It is part of the human condition and we must therefore be prepared to encounter it. What nurses may not want to admit is:

'It terrifies me.'
'It totally incapacitates me.'
'I don't know how to handle it.'

Although it is acceptable to own these feelings, many nurses do have a vast experience of the signs that precede violence. They can learn to act upon these and gain the skills for effective intervention.

HOSTILITY

Hostility is not only disruptive to the smooth running of the ward or department, but it is difficult for nurses to cope with over long periods of time, and it increases stress. It can make us feel ineffective because it incapacitates us; we can feel damaged by it and become cynical or defensive. Often, hostility is only obvious when out of control.

Hostility deserves special consideration because it is often a label attached to the difficult or disruptive patient and his family. I am interested as to why nurses in particular respond so defensively to hostility, or regard it as inappropriate.

When hostilities simmer and intensify, and no constructive outlets are available, we know that this is damaging and increases vulnerability. The patient role, by its very nature, is a vulnerable one, and the internalization of strong and hostile feelings by the patient make him increasingly more vulnerable. There is already an unequal balance of power — if the patient feels he has no control over what happens to him and he feels under attack, he will become hostile. We sense it, we see it in his eyes or hear it in conversation with him. We need to know about it.

We can intellectualize about hostility, and know what should happen, but when hostility emerges we find it unacceptable. It is a spanner in the works and will interfere with all our plans and ideas. It becomes a slap in the face or a kick in the teeth.

Bryn Davis (1984) in his work on the nurse's perception of the patient, makes some very pertinent observations. He points out that nursing has moved to being concerned with the whole patient, individualised care and nurse-patient relationships being important. Despite this his studies show that there is still evidence that nurses tend to deal with types of behaviour, types of people and types of disease. Then, their perception of the patient and the labels provided by others, particularly by other senior health professionals, influence their behaviour.

Hostility is related to stress, conflict and regression; the problem is that it is also related to violence, destruction and cruelty, which are all unacceptable. When hostility is attached to resentment, bitterness and conflict, we may be able to sympathise. But if we are to encounter patients who are vulnerable, threatened, scared or anxious, we must also encounter hostility in them.

HOSTILITY IN THE EMERGENCY DEPARTMENT

Nurses in this department become familiar with the unpredictable nature of the work and changes in pace and demand. They are more at ease with ambiguity and crisis. They deal with extremes. Some patients present with trivial injuries, others with overwhelming injuries that lead to their death. The nurses here face helplessness and hopelessness, and all the evils of society, and all its misfits. They learn to adapt to all this.

Imagine you have never been in this sort of situation before and you are in the waiting area of the department. Not only do you have to cope with being confronted with all this, but you also have your own reasons for being there as a patient or the relative of one. Many patients and relatives are sickened and angered by what they see. They will witness staff responding differently to each patient and family without knowing the whole story. They will not understand the system of priorities. When the Department is very busy it will appear chaotic, and they will wonder if it is all under control. Where does the patient, their loved one, fit into all this?

'Will he get the care he needs?'
'Will they get lost in the system?'
'Will they be identified with the misfits?'

The patient then becomes hostile and difficult. We have discussed why hostility emerges from within him, but below are listed factors within the Department which can produce this hostility and which we can modify or be aware of, and then act upon.

1. Waiting

Demand changes suddenly and patients with minor injuries will have to wait while life-threatening problems are dealt with first. Our initial assessment of some of the more minor injuries is not done once only — we reassess the patient and look for changes. This produces further contact with him, and gives an opportunity to explain any delay. A notice giving length of expected delay should be kept up-to-date. Giving information will clarify many perplexities for patients.

2. Separation from family

Doctors need privacy to see patients, because without it there cannot be a total exchange of information. An example of this is the unmarried pregnant teenage girl with waiting parents. Care must be taken to ascertain whether the patient has family or friends waiting, and who they are and where they are. If they discover the patient has been on a ward for the past hour and they have been forgotten, they will be angry. Separation, for whatever reason, needs to be explained. Regular contact, under these circumstances, will be useful.

3. Pain

Pain increases if the patient is kept waiting for long periods of time or is isolated. Sometimes, hostility is the only response a patient can make when pain is severe.

4. Noise

This adds to the general feeling of disorder, People need to shout to be heard. Shouting becomes equated with hostility. Find ways of reducing noise and of providing diversions. Music, video and magazines, and special waiting areas for children, with a blackboard and toys, are all used to this end.

5. Lack of understanding of the system

'Why did he come here after I did, but get seen first?' This is a question frequently asked and the system of priorities needs to be explained, without giving away the diagnosis of the other patients. Most departments have special areas for eye or ear problems, for plaster work or for suturing, and demand in these areas will fluctuate. Some days, it seems, everyone appears to need the eye room. Explain these problems.

6. Failure to act upon behavioural signs

If you ask the nursing staff to identify who will become hostile or difficult if kept waiting, they will do so accurately. They will have acquired skills in interpreting verbal and behavioural signs, although many would deny this. The problem is that staff fail to act upon this information, or are prevented from doing so by other priorities. Many will agree they have this ability but do not have the communications skill to handle it. If they do not have it, we must equip them with it.

7. Failure to share decisions with patient or family

If one is unable to control one's future or present because of decisions taken by others, one is likely to fight to be heard. Instead of asking:

   'Will you agree to come into hospital?'
we say
   'We are admitting you to hospital.'

This is the beginning of the change to a passive role for the patient. Relatives will often let you know he belongs to them and that he is not yours to simply take away. At this point hostility is often apparent.

8. Prejudice

The nurse without some prejudice to either a race, colour, creed, type of behaviour or labelled patient would be a rarity. We may feel that the prejudice is not really ours but that we have been conditioned with it from an early age. We should confront each other with these prejudices, and think about how they affect our responses and behaviour. A useful exercise may be to consider how they emerged.

9. Delay in answering enquiries

This can happen either on the telephone or when relatives appear in person. We must examine ways to locate patients quickly. A couple of minutes' wait is a long time for an anxious relative newly arrived in the Emergency Department. Explain to them that the Department is full of people, and that it will take time to locate the patient they want.

These, then, are some of the factors within the Emergency Department that can produce hostility. Many of them are about giving information, about clarifying some point which is difficult to understand fully. Some of the factors discussed need more study in order to examine ways of improving the system and care.

HOSTILITY AND DRUGS

It has long been recognised that drugs in the minor tranquill- lizer group can allow hostile and aggressive feelings to emerge. Gardos et al (1968) reported the effects of chlordiazepoxide, diazepam and oxazepam on a group of student volunteers. Although the drugs reduced anxiety there was an increase in overtly hostile and aggressive behaviour. This is discussed in Chapter 5 on attempted suicide, when the difficulties in handling the patient are considered.

OTHER THOUGHTS AND DIFFICULTIES

We must always be vigilant for the physiological responses to illness and injury which produce a change in mood and personality. Not all violent, hostile and difficult behaviour is psychological. Toxic states, drugs, trauma and other illnesses, too many to consider here, must be thought about along with the patient's previous medical history and current medication. Our considerations in this chapter have been about the psychological reasons which lead to the difficult and disruptive patient and family.

Sometimes a nurse will recognise that a patient is troubled in some way, but manages to avoid the issue. It may be that the nurse or patient is aware of where the focus is. Talking about key people in the patient's life, either at home or at work, may give clues because you may note a change in feel- ings, or become aware of the control of feelings. One anxiety of the nurse or her supervisor is that she can become too involved. One of the nurse's responsibilities will be to recognise her limitations. If you are using your crisis counselling skills it is because of an immediate problem that interferes with the well-being or recovery of your patient.

Wilson-Barnett & Fordham (1982) have demonstrated how illness is perceived as a crisis and how this needs intervention to facilitate recovery. Therefore it is an essential part of your care to intervene in this way. You can motivate the patient to seek the right kind of help and point him in the direction of where that help is. This total care will prevent many difficulties and disruptions, and although the causes of these are many and varied, we have, in this chapter, covered those which are most general.

Case study

Gerald is 61 years old and smokes like a chimney. He says it's his only pleasure in life and jokingly makes references to the fact that he never married. For 40 years he has worked as a hall porter in one of the top hotels in town, where he began as a bell boy. He loves to relate stories of the famous people who have stayed at the hotel. He tells the most outrageous tales, but discreetly and with a twinkle in his eye.

He shares a bungalow with his sister, Alice, who is single, older, and vociferous. He has had two hospital admissions, one for pneumonia and one for the removal of an ingrowing toenail. Each stay was for less than a week because he discharged himself when in hospital with pneumonia as 'too much fuss was being made about it'.

His long smoking history makes him a bit breathless but he can cope with that. However, he could not cope with the pains in his calves after walking short distances, nor with the cramps at night. He had an idea that there was something wrong with the circulation in his legs as they were often cold and blue looking. He was worried. He needed his sleep at his age and he especially needed his legs. He knew his chest was 'a bit rattly' but he could manage that. He felt better at night propped up and with his legs hanging over the edge of the bed. He often got up to make a cup of tea.

He eventually agreed to go to the doctor's because of his nagging sisters's persistence and complaints about his meanderings at night which were keeping her awake. 'Anything for a quiet life,' he thought. His doctor referred him to a surgeon at the local hospital who specialised in arterial surgery. The surgeon decided Gerald should be admitted for special X-rays, saying something about narrowed arteries and the need for an operation.

Gerald had never heard of this problem before and told his sister it was probably some new fangled idea and he was to be the guinea pig. She dismissed such an idea as preposterous, and when the card came, saying Gerald was to present for admission, she had his bag packed in no time. For 2 weeks she had prepared clean pyjamas, dressing gown and underclothes.

'I don't want you showing me up in there, so you behave yourself,' she told him.

His sister was a retired teacher, and Gerald had an idea she was enjoying getting him ready and having something different to think about. He was very much aware of, and full of dread about the fact that Alice always rose to the occasion. She took charge of him and put him in the car. He was pleased her friend Gladys was not with them, or Alice would have been even more intolerable. He insisted she stop at the local tobacconist's for his 100 cigarettes — it was actually 200 but he did not want her to know that.

As they continued the journey, she lectured him, on the subject of now being a good time to stop smoking. She went on to say that these cigarettes had to last at least 2 weeks. He knew that 200 usually lasted 5 days and that he had no plans to stay in hospital for weeks. He was weary with thinking about the whole thing, and the 'cold' he was getting made him more miserable.

The male surgical ward was bright and cheerful having just been redecorated. At the far end there was a television lounge which looked out onto lawns and flower beds. The ward was a hive of activity. Sister Griffiths was discussing various items from the ward round with the consultant when Alice entered her office and announced that Gerald was here.

'Who is Gerald?' Sister Griffiths asked, annoyed at the interruption.

'Why, Gerald Brown, of course,' replied Alice, giving Sister one of her looks.

'Wait outside, please,' Sister said, 'and staff nurse will come and get details.'

The thought that went through the minds of both those ladies was 'I am going to have trouble with her and it will have to be clear from the start that I won't stand for any nonsense.'

Staff nurse David Jones found Gerald and Alice sitting in the corridor with an uneasy look about them. Gerald had just told Alice to stop finding fault and to keep quiet. Staff nurse Jones sat down and asked for some personal details such as name and address, next of kin and home telephone number.

'Sister told us a staff nurse would attend to us, orderly,' Alice remarked curtly.

'That's me,' David said.

Alice, taken aback, was lost for words for a short time. This amused Gerald. He liked to see her caught out now and again. When David asked Gerald's religion Alice suddenly had a panic:

'Goodness, I haven't let the Minister Know! I'll go round to see him on the way home.'

'I don't want to see him,' Gerald replied.

The staff nurse left, saying he was going to organise Gerald's bed. Before he was through the door, Alice was admonishing Gerald:

'Don't show me up by saying things like that.'

Staff nurse Jones suddenly reappeared and told Gerald they would finish the questionnaire and other details when he was settled in to the ward. Alice offered to answer them for him, but David declined the offer and gave her a book with details of the hospital visiting times. Even Alice realised this was a hint to leave.

After showing Gerald round the ward, David took Gerald to his bed. He was next to a kindly, old man who was 3 days post-op. from a hernia operation. David knew he would put Gerald at ease, but was concerned about the overtalkative appendicectomy patient who was on his left.

Gerald was tucked up in bed, and looking all neat and clean when Alice visited in the afternoon.

'What did the Doctor find when he examined you on admission?' she demanded.

'Nothing,' was Gerald's reply.

'Didn't you ask him?' asked Alice.

'No, why should I?'

'Its your body, Gerald, that's why. You must learn to open your mouth now and again. It's a sign of an active brain, is an enquiring mind . . .'

Gerald's thoughts were at the hotel. They always said they couldn't manage without him but they would soon learn to. That Fred Jackson was just waiting to get his job . . .

'Are you listening to me, Gerald? If you don't want to know, I do!'

Sister Griffiths had seen that look of disdain and boredom on patient's faces before, when visitors were unwelcome.

'Gerald Brown has had enough of her,' she thought, and no sooner had this entered her head than she saw Alice heading towards her office, looking very business-like.

'Now what have you got planned for Gerald? You must keep me in the picture.'

'Very little at the moment,' was Sister's reply. She then added, 'Gerald will keep you informed.'

Alice left, but that evening she visited her brother, along with her friend Gladys, which was all Gerald needed. He was not feeling too well — his chest was bothering him and he had a bit of a temperature — and matters were made worse by these two talking non-stop to each other, pausing only occasionally to whisper questions about what was wrong with his fellow patients.

Five days later little had changed. Things were held up because of Gerald's slight temperature. The X-rays were cancelled because the machine broke down. The loud-mouthed surgical expert in the next bed had been discharged. In his place was a chap whose skin was bright yellow and looked deathly. His visitors, especially one woman, were near to tears all the time, and spoke in strained, controlled voices. On his other side, Gerald's only confidant had gone home, and was replaced by a teenager who listened to the radio all day. As a result, Gerald visited the television room a lot, where he could smoke, but Sister opened all the windows constantly, to clear the air, so he felt very uneasy about it. Privately she had said it was no good doing all this work on his legs if he continued to smoke.

Quietly, Gerald listened to everything and gave very little

feedback. On the seventh day, even though David Jones was nearby, Gerald went up to the lad in the next bed and said 'For God's sake, take those damned earphones off and speak for once.' before he stalked off to the television room.

The injection of dye for the X-ray, and all the apparatus surrounding Gerald, made the afternoon a thoroughly disturbing one for him. Alice and Gladys visited in the evening and Alice told staff nurse Jenny Simms that all the staff were incompetent for allowing her to visit when he was in X-ray. Jenny found her difficult to handle, and Alice returned jubilant to Gladys after the outburst:

'They need telling. Gerald won't do it. He just sits there saying nothing.'

That night Gerald slept badly, developed cramp in his legs and had a great need to walk about. The night nurses were busy and the relatives of the yellow man on his right arrived at 2 in the morning, all crying. Gerald knew he was a nuisance when he asked for some pain killers. All that talk about his operation and X-ray by the doctors might just as well have been double Dutch. He had no idea what they were talking about and could not follow the explanations at all. He'd end up like this poor devil in the bed beside him — half dead.

Gerald must have fallen asleep because when he woke again at 5.00 am he was screened off and he heard some activity on his right. The two nurses were talking in hushed voices. He looked out round the screen and the other patients were also screened off. Suddenly a nurse appeared:

'Go back to bed. Hurry up. We'll be late with the morning tea.'

When the lights came up, the bed on his right was empty and neatly set out with clean sheets and counterpane for the next admission. When the tea came round, Gerald asked what time his neighbouring patient had died. The reply was:

'No questions. Now Gerald, how many sugars do you take? It's not like you to ask questions, Gerald.'

Gerald's thought was 'No, and it's not like you to answer them!'

He was restless before the consultant's round. Sitting only for short periods, he walked to and fro between his bed and the television lounge. The lawn and flowers looked bright through the window. The hotel garden would look good now.

He felt stupid as tears welled up in his eyes. Just then David Jones touched his arm.

'You looked worried, Mr Brown, and now you're upset.'

Gerald gripped his arm and was about to share his feelings when Sister interrupted to ask him to return to bed for the ward round.

Gerald was told by the consultant when his operation would be, and Gerald's only question, put falteringly, was would he guarantee it would work? This produced mild amusement and a smart answer about a 12-month warranty.

Alice's visit that afternoon was worse than ever. She mentioned numerous people she would inform of his operation date. In fact she continued to talk, not quite believing it was Gerald's voice shouting:

'Shut your mouth, woman!'

There was silence on the ward, suddenly. Patients and visitors all looked in his direction.

'What are you looking at?' he shouted.

Alice jumped up.

'Gerald, please behave yourself.'

'Shut up and go away,' he replied loudly.

Sister arrived, saying 'You're not doing yourself any good.'

Gerald continued to shout about how everyone else knew what was good for him, as he took his clothes from the locker and started to get dressed.

Alice wailed and cried, and was taken off to the office. Sister had the strong impression that she would be better dealing with Alice, and staff nurse David Jones was sent to talk to Gerald. They went to the ward kitchen, and sat and had tea, and David said:

'Now, you were about to tell me something this morning . . .'

QUESTIONS ON THE CASE STUDY

1. What indications were there that Gerald was not coping with his feelings?
2. How would you have handled Alice?
3. At what stage would you have intervened with Gerald, to enable him to share his real feelings?

160 / *Caring in Crisis*

4. a. Make a list of the factors that prevented staff from
      responding to Gerald's emotional needs.
   b. Discuss this list and the changes you would make to
      have emotional needs met.

REFERENCES

Aitken S 1984 The patient as enemy. 'Changes' 2:2
Davies B D 1984 What is the nurse's perception of the patient? In:
  Skevington S (ed) Understanding nurses. Wiley, Chichester
Gardos E, Dimascio A, Salzman C, Shader R I 1968 Differential actions of
  chlordiazepoxide and oxazepam on hostility. Archives of General
  Psychiatry 18 (June)
Kelly M P, May D 1982 Good and bad patients: A review of the literature
  and a theoretical critique. Journal of Advanced Nursing 7(2): 147–156
Roberts D 1984 Non-verbal communication: popular and unpopular
  patients. In: Faulkener A (ed) Communication. Recent Advances in
  Nursing Series. Churchill Livingstone, Edinburgh
Wilson-Barnett J, Fordham M 1982 Recovery from illness. Wiley, Chichester

9

Staff stress

Case study

Jenny was a staff nurse in her second year on an intensive care unit. She was very much aware of the fact that she had learnt so much more since she had qualified, not only about the technical side of nursing and the physical care of patients. What she really valued was learning to cope and making decisions under stressful conditions. What she wanted more than anything was to be able to cope in a crisis, because she felt she had gained a great deal of knowledge about herself in her care of families in crisis.

Her new knowledge made her re-evaluate herself, her family and her friends, and had altered her outlook on life. She often thought about the way she had grown and learnt from the many situation of pain, suffering and disintegration she had seen. It was a valued and important part of her time on the intensive care unit.

Suddenly she became aware of changes that were occurring in her life and which distressed her — she was impatient and angry with minor difficulties and her sudden tearfulness worried her and her colleagues. She knew they were anxious about confronting her with her conflict. She loved helping people but hated what it did to her feelings. When she realised there was no-one in the unit that she could talk to, she was angry. She wanted support; they wanted her to increase her workload. Small demands became overwhelming and she felt her managers did not care. Her resentment at what her commitment was doing to her feelings increased her bitterness. She became aware of feeling helpless and impotent.

All that caring and giving had taken its toll. All that outpouring, without anything taking its place and refilling her, had drained her. Instead of feeling that her contacts with patients, families, colleagues and work were meaningful experiences, she felt they were to be avoided. They damaged, they led to feelings of disintegration. Her attempts to defend herself against this prevented people from getting close — this was too risky.

Eventually, Jenny left, sad and disillusioned, with the awful feeling that instead of gaining from her work she had lost something vital to her needs. She felt damaged.

There was a time when a nurse was someone who took temperatures, applied bandages and nursed and nurtured patients. Let us hope that nurses continue to do this, along with the wider role they have assumed with its greater responsibilities. This change was necessary if nursing was to progress. A background in areas of science, psychology, biology, chemistry, microbiology, anatomy, physiology, sociology and much more, has widened our horizons and our knowledge. This explosion in knowledge has created a need for more advanced educational programmes and practices. It has also increased our status in multidisciplinary teams at the same time as cutbacks and the re-defining of boundaries have meant increased workloads.

This change in role and status is, for the most part, rewarding and stimulating, but it brings with it increased stress. We all know now how useful stress can be in effecting work and change. What happens if the stress becomes crisis, or if we are overwhelmed by it? Will it be recognised? Or what about the many occasions when it is recognised but colleagues fail to respond? Many feel they do not have the skills, and find it a frightening problem to deal with.

Not only do problems at work loom large because they are disruptive of our work plans, but we can also identify with patients' problems, which will increase our own difficulties. The whole situation can take on an overwhelming identity, and if it is not dealt with by confronting the nurse, her demoralisation and damage will spread to others.

Can any of you recognise the burnt-out ward sister? The one who copes but with emotional detachment, and is insensitive to patient and staff needs. The cynicisms you hear from her, day after day, her withdrawal and working in isolation, go along with her lack of vision and ideals and she is rigid and unapproachable. She denies having any personal needs when many of her problems stem from her denying her own emotional existence. Although we can all recognise this person, let us first try to identify crisis within ourselves and our colleagues in an objective way. We will do this partly by reflecting ways in which crisis becomes apparent in the nurse's attitudes to her patients, and partly by considering other aspects of her working life.

IDENTIFYING STAFF CRISIS

Below is a list of attributes that can indicate strong feelings of disillusionment and crisis:

1. Labelling patients

This can be an indication of having to categorize patients, and is often judgemental. The nurse feels the need to put some order into the situation.

2. Unappreciated

Feelings that colleagues or the management are unaware of her predicament or choose to ignore it. She is resentful that her contribution is devalued or not appreciated. In more severe states of burn-out these feelings turn into paranoia — feelings that people, the system and the patients are against her.

3. Intolerance

Tolerance of others is not one of the virtues of a burnt-out nurse. She is cynical about her work or about new ideas.

Sarcastic remarks abound and she finds her work un-imaginative and boring.

4. Exhaustion

The nurse complains of feeling weak and sluggish. There is a marked loss of energy and a feeling of weariness. This is difficult to accept as the nurse may have had lots of energy before. It produces perplexity and anxiety.

5. Illness and absenteeism

If illness and absenteeism are associated with the previous or following factors, crisis or burn-out should be considered. It will be difficult for the nurse to admit that anything is wrong or that she cannot cope. Illness will be more acceptable.

6. Feeling professionally inadequate

In this competitive world it is difficult to admit to feeling professionally inadequate. There is so much change and so many new ideas, and so much that the nurse needs to be aware of, especially when she is surrounded by students. She needs time and enthusiasm to keep abreast of all this.

It is easy to feel left behind and lacking in the skills or knowledge to continue with many aspects of her work. For some nurses, admitting this would be difficult because they would have to face it themselves and in some areas it would be unacceptable to management.

7. Avoiding patients

Avoiding direct interaction with patients and finding them irritating and distracting can be the start of the nurse's feeling bad about herself. Most nurses will be aware that this is happening because they soon feel guilty about it.

8. Unrealistic wishes

When two or three patients presenting with cardiac arrests arrive in the Emergency Department within 20 or 30 minutes of each other, we all wish they could be spaced out more appropriately, say, one every hour. If this kind of wishing stays with the nurse and begins to preoccupy her, she is being unrealistic. If she complains persistently that patients or their relatives never do the right thing when faced with an emergency she is being equally unrealistic as she is when she wonders why people cannot be sensible all the time, like she is. If this is the case, she needs to look at the next category too.

9. Omnipotent and overinvolved

'I will not allow anyone else to help because they will make a mess of it. Nobody can do it as well as I can.' When she has to do everything herself in order to get the work done properly, she is failing somewhere. Lack of resources may be a problem, but there may be an unwillingness to hand over some of the power. Some people will have to stay late because they feel that they alone can finish the task, rather than because of lack of resources.

10. Change overwhelms

The nurse should ask herself about her response to change. It should disturb her enough to enable her to respond to its challenge. Some change has dramatic implications, other change needs minor adjustment. If any change produces feelings of being swamped or overwhelmed, this can indicate that her coping mechanisms are being stretched.

These, then, are some of the indications that a nurse is in crisis or has burnt out. Before we move on to other signs, or ways to cope, we should consider briefly what coping is.

WHAT IS COPING?

In simple terms coping is our way of dealing with change, and our response to that change. Lazarus (1966), in his studies about coping behaviour, describes two aspects of coping:

The first aspect explores how we alter the situation which is stressful or has the potential for crisis. To achieve this we may try to alter the nature of the situation itself. This may involve getting someone to alter his responses or feelings towards the stressful factors.

The second aspect of coping is to alter or deal with our thoughts, in order to deal with the stress. This may not involve any change in the stressors, but it does concern the way we manage them. Stressors can become tolerable by avoidance, drinking, smoking, taking up voluntary work or some other diversion. In this way we manage the stress or crisis.

Coping, then, is how a person handles demands and conflicts. It involves how he tolerates these or minimises them. These demands and conflicts will be from both within and without, and the coping will be the ways he handles his own feelings, thoughts and bodily responses, and at the same time the thoughts, feelings and bodily responses of others.

There is no one way of coping with a given situation. We have already said we may change it or manage it. The response to it depends upon a person's previous experiences, personality, relationships with others, and environment. Coping is considering all these dynamics.

We have looked at the signs of crisis, and what it means to cope. Now we will look at solving the problem.

FINDING A FOCUS FOR INTERVENTION

Begin by identifying the main focus of the stress in the work. If an attempt is made in a short time to sort out all the nurse's problems, which have built up over the years, you could fail. The other problem with this approach is that it is so unrealistic as to have an air of magic about it. We want to prevent attempts at unrealistic goals from the start, and to demystify our approach.

Having decided on a main source of stress or dissatisfaction, the suggested responses may be of help. All require the motivation to change and manage one's feelings and reactions. Some nurses will need to be confronted about what will be left if their dissatisfaction is removed, and whether they want what will be left. Being satisfied and stimulated will require something else of them, and perhaps even a fundamental change in their behaviour.

Below are some responses to problems which may be considered after the nurse has confirmed she wants the challenge of change. Some responses will deal with several of the symptoms listed previously.

POSSIBLE RESPONSES TO STAFF CRISIS

1. *The nurse could ask for a move.* A lateral transfer or change in shift or working hours may be all that is needed. This move from a well-worn routine with the same people may be all the stimulus she needs to be re-motivated. Working with a different type of patient or considering whether she wants a longer or shorter transaction with patients may also be useful.

The move will mean new demands and responses and may mean some re-education. The nurse should be sure, before she makes this move, that she does not want to move away from nursing altogether. Initially, the thought of a complete change may produce anxiety and more stress. The alternative is working for change in the situation she is in, or managing the stress in an alternative way. She should ask herself if any of this is possible.

2. *Seek further education.* Not only will this increase her knowledge, but it will give the nurse more self-confidence. No longer will she be continually catching up with everyone else who is one step ahead of her, she will be alongside them. The confidence that this produces is powerful enough to make her want to maintain that progress. A greater understanding means that she will offer the patients more support. They are less likely to confront her with questions or areas she cannot deal with, and which leave her feeling inadequate. Continuing education plays an important part in keeping us all stimulated.

3. *Examine her life outside work.* How she uses her spare time, or if she has enough of it, are areas to be examined here. In her leisure time she may spend too long with colleagues, discussing work. There are many areas to look at in finding ways to unwind — some are more overt ways of

discharging hostility, such as physical exercise: squash, running, basketball or judo. There are other less energetic, activities like yoga, meditation, playing a musical instrument, or joining an amateur dramatic group.

If there is some particular personal or relationship difficulty, the nurse should do something about it, perhaps by seeking some counselling before it does her damage. Many people suddenly become aware of difficulties they have had for many years when these begin to interfere with their occupation. This problem can be an insidious, demoralising process. Now that she is confronted with or becomes aware of its strength, she should tackle it.

In examining her life outside work she should also consider her lifestyle. For nurses, many activities involve a time factor, and the pace of work can spill over into their personal life. They should take time to eat, travel, relax and sleep. Few things are as urgent as we think they are. Is what she is working so hard for, what she really wants?

4. *Do not be unrealistic.* Some patients, relatives and staff will not match up to her expectations. Some will have decided from the start that they do not wish to. Treatment plans and programmes will be disrupted and unsuitable, and will need change and readjustment. Nurse are dealing with people, unique individuals, which is one of the attractions of the work. These people may let her down, and her plans may go awry. She is being unrealistic if she becomes too disturbed and damaged by this.

5. *Contribute to and encourage support systems.* Some people who work in high stress areas recognise the need for support and discussion groups. Suggest, support and encourage this by sharing your fears, frustrations and anxieties. If no such group exists, make space in your working time to allow and encourage the discharge of feelings of frustration. If you notice someone having a particularly difficult time, make a point of encouraging them to talk or allow them to have a break.

It seems strange, but it is necessary, to remind nurses they must care for one another.

If none of these have anything to offer the nurse, she may want to seek a change in her career. The alternative is that she becomes so sad, so miserable that none of the above will motivate her. She may also be unable to find a focus even with your help, or she may be unable to concentrate on the focus of her problems and may feel there is no answer at all to them. This indicates a more serious long-term difficulty which needs psychiatric or psychotherapeutic intervention.

UNIT CRISIS

Recent research has highlighted how some areas of acute and critical care are far more likely to give rise to stress and crisis in the staff. Boxall (1983), in studying stress in neonatal units, listed the key issues as staff shortages, deaths, relapses and coping with handicaps. Environmental conditions, such as heat, lack of space, noise and equipment breakdowns, were also classed as stress-producing factors.

In the renal unit staff and patients can develop long-term relationships which become very significant because of the decisions being taken and ever-changing circumstances. Staff can experience with the patient the wait for a donor kidney and then the trauma of rejection. Often, nurses are included in the life and death decisions that are taken in relation to continued treatment or transplant. Pritchard (1982), in his observations on the stress of working in renal units, suggested the stress was related to roles. He found a disturbing discrepancy between usual expectations and actual experience. This focus is certainly useful in the preparation of nurses for these units, and in pointing out areas to work with.

Ryan (1982) describes how the environment of the Intensive Care Unit effects staff working in this highly charged, stressful and potentially critical atmosphere. Adequate rest facilities and efficient air conditioning are really valued. Ryan shows how, when the nurse is barrier nursing in side wards and is faced with all the equipment of the unit, she can feel isolated and inadequate. Lack of windows is another factor often cited as a cause of stress.

Although it is the high-tech units which have been identified here, stress and burn-out occur in other areas, particularly in those associated with death and dying and pain.

David Potterton (1984) in his interview with Barbara

Saunders, Senior Sister in charge of the Terminal Support Team at St Thomas' Hospital, London, discussed the effect on nurses of witnessing pain. It was said that this drives nurses to smoke, become ill, leave or become detatched from the patients. The well-motivated nurse would try to seek help from others or find ways of helping herself.

I hope we have the right structure and people to meet these needs in our staff. If we accept that some units are more prone to crisis in staff, it is important that we learn to recognise the onset of crisis.

SIGNS OF UNIT CRISIS

1. Frequent complaints from patients or other departments may indicate fragmentation or even lack of policy. They may also indicate a failure to deal adequately with grievances because staff no longer care what sort of reputation their unit has. A feeling that someone else is always to blame suggests discord.

2. Increased absenteeism and sickness may indicate a particular pressure at the time, such as staff shortages or discontentment. Leaving your colleagues to cope when you have poor justification to do so indicates a lack of cohesion and comradeship. Included in this area should be persistent bad timekeeping. Is this a sign of lack of commitment?

3. Poor co-operation about sticking to policy or plans again questions commitment and suggests discord.

4. Changes in staff, routine or policy can produce disturbances. One sign of unit problems is when small changes begin to present as large problems.

5. Sub-groups which gossip and quarrel should give cause for concern, especially if people are excluded and scapegoating results. If one person's name is frequently associated with many problems, you should ask yourself what is happening.

Most units will show some of these signs, especially if the pace is subject to sudden changes, and life and death questions are involved. We should, nevertheless, make efforts to relieve tensions and factors that include stress and crisis.

PREVENTION OF STAFF CRISIS

1. Know your strengths and weaknesses. Hopefully your supervisor will be aware of them.
2. Communicate at all levels, and reappraise channels of communication.
3. Recognise individual skills and strengths, and give staff and yourself the room to grow.
4. An awareness of goals and expectations deals with questions of being unrealistic. This approach to expectations should be at individual and unit level.
5. Roles are not static. Re-evaluate them periodically.
6. By initiating awareness to staff crisis and stress, and responding to it, you set a good role model.
7. Recognise and validate positive contribution and encourage enthusiasm.
8. Continuing education maintains enthusiasm and interest.

MANAGERS FEEL STRESS TOO

We should not forget that managing is a stressful occupation and also has the potential for crisis. It is a frequent assumption amongst nurses that all the stress centres around the patient/nurse transaction. You will have heard how well some managers operate when responding to crisis and that this is known as crisis management, but the idea that this comes easily to managers suggests an ignorance of and cynicism about their role, although we have already noted that some stress will be useful in order to initiate action and innovation.

The manager's position in the hierarchical structure determines the direction from which the stress comes. If you are at the top, demands will come from below and you may be expected to come up with all the answers. The first-line manager will feel pressures from above and below, and will feel he has little power to make decisions.

Another realistic anxiety for managers is that roles can change quickly especially when reorganisation takes place. As managers cost more money, it can easily be in this area that changes and cuts are made. Many managers will have to make decisions about where and when to move up the ladder. Or is it safer to stay where he is? These moves mean disruption for spouse and, in some cases, children.

Alongside all this is a responsibility for hundreds of people, a service and a large budget. The manager's judgement needs to be sound under these pressures and he needs to be effective. Now, if all that sounds a heavy load, who do you think the manager can talk to when the going gets tougher? It certainly can be a lonely place at the top. When you are perceived as being strong and a leader, it is more difficult in many ways to admit to feeling pressure, lack of direction and weakness. In our many blanket condemnations of managers, we should spare a thought for the fact that they too experience crisis.

We examined how we can look at the focus of crisis in ourselves or in a colleague, in order to alleviate it. We then explored various responses that are useful on an individual level. One of these responses suggested a contribution to and encouragement of support systems, an example of which was group support. I had some experience of these critical care areas in the USA, and, since many British-trained nurses have little experience of how groups work as a support system, we will consider the value of this intervention and how to enable the group to function.

GROUP WORK AS A SUPPORT SYSTEM

In critical care units such as Intensive Care, Accident and Emergency and other specialised areas, staff are faced with many aspects of stress and crisis. They may have to make rapid decisions in crisis situations, adapt to changes in pace and demand, and cope with extremes of feelings and emotions. It is not at all unusual for hostility and aggression or scape-goating to occur between disciplines when under pressure. Consequently many staff members feel damaged or incapacitated by the feelings that emerge, and some will have difficulty in confronting the issues in the unit or elsewhere. The internalization of the feelings, and the individual's inability to deal with these issues, are unhealthy. For this reason, a time is set aside for the sole purpose of airing views and feelings.

The fact that this can be done in working time in a staff group has special implications. It means that the management recognises the stress and the need to share and confront it, and it shows they are concerned with the cohesion and effectiveness of the team. If the group is multidisciplinary, it means that everyone's contribution is recognised and that common fears, problems and anxieties are shared. It endorses the value of the teams interaction, to all oisciplines.

This group of people with a common aim will need to be clear that it will be beneficial to operate like this and they may need assurances as to how safe it is to expose themselves in this way. It should be clear that the aim is to support, increase empathy, and resolve emotive issues that occur due to the nature of the work.

Members of the group are going to form impressions about other members. They will like or dislike, trust or regard them with suspicion. They may wonder whether the rewards will justify the risks that may need to be taken. It is to be hoped that together, they will find solutions to problems and will air views and feelings in safety — and from the start it will be necessary to define the goals and for members to discuss their expectations of the group.

This form of group support should not be regarded as an economy of effort, but as an effective way of offering support and strength. It is not a substitute for, or a way into, individual counselling. Some groups have rules, and it may reduce staff anxiety about the group if everyone has a printed copy of the rules and aims of the group. These ground rules may proyide an ice-breaker in the opening discussion. A leader can be chosen to start the group off and once established the task can be shared — some may feel happier if the leader has experience of group work.

I have found the ground rules of Gendlin & Beebe (1968) Particularly useful, as they enable members to feel safe and offer some guidelines about what is and is not allowed. The overall philosophy of these rules also emphasises how an increased empathy can be achieved. Although they were designed for a sensitivity group, they are in many ways universally applicable.

Table 9.1 Ground rules for group sessions (Gendlin & Beebe 1968)

1. Everyone who is here belongs here just because he is here and for no other reason.

2. For each person, what is true is determined by what is in him, what he directly feels and finds making sense in himself and the way he lives inside himself.

3. Our first purpose is to make contact with each other. Everything else we want or need comes second.

4. We try to be as honest as possible and to express ourselves as we really are and really feel — just as much as we can.

5. We listen for the person inside, living and feeling.

6. We listen to everyone.

7. The group leader is responsible for two things only: he protects the belonging of every member, and he protects their being heard if this is getting lost.

8. Realism — if we know things are a certain way, we do not pretend they are not that way.

9. What we say here is confidential. No one will repeat anything said here outside the group, unless it concerns only himself. This applies not just to obviously private things but to everything. If the individual concerned wants others to known something, he can always tell them himself.

10. Decisions made by the group need everyone taking part in some way.

11. New members become members because they walk in and remain. Whoever is here belongs.

After 4–6 weeks, a period of evaluation would be useful for a weekly group.

BURN-OUT ASSOCIATED WITH CHANGES IN NURSING PRACTICE

Previously, we have asked questions about change when looking for a focus for intervention, but change in itself can be disturbing and even overwhelming. If you are happy with the status quo, you will not welcome change:

We have suffered several major changes over the past few years. Why do I say 'suffered'? Some of them have been constructive changes that have enhanced patient care and increased the nurse's knowledge and status.

We can make changes easier by preparing staff for it. They

will need a space to air views about the change and the ideas behind it. They will need to discuss how security is threatened by it. We can encourage a positive attitude towards change by inviting ideas on ways of introducing it. Sudden change is difficult to handle so we must therefore allow time for gradual alterations.

The reasons for the change need to be made clear, even if staff do not agree with them. Perplexity and searching for answers and clarification reinforces negative responses. Persistent complaining about or negation of new ideas and innovation can become an acceptable way of coping for some members of staff, and should be discouraged.

Some changes, by their very philosophy, can result in crisis for nurses, e.g. those concerned with political or financial restraints. The Royal College of Nursing Report 'Nurse Alert' (1984) gives several examples of the stress and crisis induced in nurses by the manpower and financial cuts. I wonder whether, when such plans are made and initiated, anyone considers what support and counselling services will be available to the people whose burden is increased or whose job is axed.

Other changes, such as those in the nursing process, are made to improve patient care and our approach to the whole patient. When we were allocated tasks for each patient, our concept of the total person must have been fragmented. Our increased awareness of the patient means we are more able to identify with him. This removes some of our defences, and our increased awareness of the disturbance on the part of the patient and his family, as a result of his illness, must increase our stress.

We are now taught to be more aware of the overall implications of the patient's illness, and this must surely result in more difficulties for the nurse emotionally. Although this approach may be more desirable, it would be equally appropriate to teach nurses how to cope with their increased emotional vulnerability.

We seek more autonomy, but we cannot have this without more accountability. This change in our role means we have to expose our practice of nursing for examination by others. We will have to account for what we do and why we do it and the philosophy behind it.

If this sounds like a burden, it is one we have invited. It can be challenging, exciting and demanding, and all these feelings can stimulate or overwhelm.

The changing face of nursing has some very positive aspects. We must also be aware of, and be prepared for, the crisis and stress this change can produce.

QUESTIONS FOR DISCUSSION

1. Refer to the case study at the start of the chapter:
   a. What signs that Jenny was in crisis could her colleagues have acted upon?
   b. How can stress be prevented in units where it has a high incidence?
2. How have recent changes in nursing increased the nurse's vulnerability?
3. Discuss the statement:
   'Nurses have a personal responsibility to keep themselves healthy.'

REFERENCES

Boxall J 1983 Stress and the nurse in neonatal units. Midwives' Chronicle 96:1151
Gendlin E T, Beebe J 1968 An experimental approach to group therapy. Journal of Research and Development in Education 1: 19–29
Lazarus R 1966 Psychological stress and the coping process. McGraw Hill, New York
Nurse Alert 1984 Royal College of Nursing, London
Potterton D 1984 The pain of cancer nursing. Nursing Times 80:11
Pritchard M 1982 Psychological pressure in a renal unit. British Journal of Hospital Medicine 27:5
Ryan D W 1982 The morbidity of intensive care. Hospital Update 8:10

10

Conclusion

There is a need for specialist helpers to deal with the numerous complexities of human problems. For nurses these problems are part of the whole patient: for some the problems will be minor whereas for others they will be a major part of the patient's focus.

We cannot be part of the healing process and ignore the psychological problems; our need to respond to these problems is as great as the patient's need for them to be met.

The purpose of this book is to examine the helping process and to provide a framework within which the nurse can work. This helps to prevent the nurse becoming overwhelmed by the task and to work within his/her limitations. I hope the book will arm you with some skills and increase your knowledge of the principles that underlie crisis.

My references to various pieces of research are by no means a comprehensive list but are, I believe, relevant to this work. I hope they will encourage you to read further.

Nursing has made great leaps into the realms of technology, but we are also searching for ways to improve personal communication and human relations, although sadly in these areas, improvement is often simply an outpouring of new skills and ideas from the nurse. We must continue to explore ways of helping the patient to find, within himself, the resources to cope. We must continue to work with our patients' potential. I hope you will feel the book focuses on normal people, or patients if you prefer, who, when faced with some overwhelming problem can be offered some means of coping.

I emphasise communication skills in a crisis. A fundamental problem in all human relations is reaching each other successfully. The key reasons why you can provide help are:

1. you are in the useful position of being the patient's nurse which is a position of trust
2. you are a person, an individual.

The book concentrates on your becoming a more aware and effective person, which, along with crisis-counselling skills, will help you to become more in tune with your patient's needs and with the outcome he expects. You can therefore understand, comfort and then act.

As this text is based on my 20 years' practice and study, it is obviously part of me and my philosophy. I make no apologies for that. I recognise that it may, at times, seem complex and that you may find it controversial but there are no neat, clear, well-defined answers to our patients' crises.

I set out to describe the process of crisis and consider the process of intervention. The areas dealt with are considered in the light of cultural and current social needs and problems. These will change, along with other areas of nursing.

I hope the areas we have explored and discussed will help you and your patients to attain personal goals and will strengthen their ability to cope with life.

It is difficult to solve personal problems alone — we all need somebody to assume a kind of help-giving relationship with us. For a patient or his family, who is in a better position to do this than the nurse?

Index